S0-BCX-068

SAINT JOSEPH'S UNIVERSITY

DEPARTMENT OF ENGLISH

TO:	Writers and users of *Pocket Keys for Writers*
FROM:	Owen W. Gilman, Jr.
	Chair, Department of English
DATE:	May 14, 2002
RE:	Getting the most from *Pocket Keys for Writers*

Beginning with the fall 2002 semester, the Department of English will require *Pocket Keys for Writers* in all introductory-level writing courses. In selecting this handbook, we were impressed with the way Ann Raimes presents a wide range of issues relevant for developing writers. Raimes organizes her book sensibly. You can easily find thoughtful guidance on everything from proper use of the comma to prescribed documentation formats for internet sources in academic projects.

Pocket Keys for Writers will help you in your growth as a writer in **all** of your courses at Saint Joseph's University. Keep this book handy whenever you work on a writing project. When revising, consult the handbook regularly to determine correct usage. No matter what discipline you study, the handbook will be helpful. There is a chapter on the Modern Language Association (MLA) style for English classes. For research-based writing in the social sciences, turn to the section on American Psychological Association (APA) style. If you have a math or science writing assignment, review the material on style as recommended by the Council of Biology Editors (CBE). Throughout your program of study, *Pocket Keys for Writers* should travel everywhere with you. It will be a good companion, answering your composition questions and guiding you to good decisions as you develop as a writer through a variety of assignments.

Writers learn by writing. Your learning will gain power and depth as you write. Each assignment will call for the utmost in integrity. Writing well takes time. It isn't easy work, but the rewards are great in terms of personal development and satisfaction.

Do not be tempted by short cuts. The section on plagiarism in *Pocket Keys for Writers* spells out your responsibility. If you claim credit for another writer's work, you compromise the opportunity to learn and also violate Saint Joseph's Academic Honesty Policy, which is reprinted in the first part of *Pocket Keys for Writers*. The consequences for such unethical behavior are appropriately stringent.

In your goal to become a confident and successful writer, *Pocket Keys for Writers* will help you achieve splendid progress. I wish you much success.

PHILADELPHIA'S JESUIT UNIVERSITY

5600 CITY AVENUE · PHILADELPHIA, PENNSYLVANIA 19131-1395 · 610/660-1880

SAINT JOSEPH'S UNIVERSITY

RE: Academic Honesty Policy

Dear Saint Joseph University Student:

    I am the chair of the Academic Honesty Board, which is a body composed of seventeen (17) students and faculty members who hear cases involving alleged violations of the Academic Honesty Policy.

    The most common violation of Saint Joseph's University's Academic Honesty Policy in recent years is plagiarism. More students are accused of "…the appropriation of information, ideas, or the language of other persons or writers and the submission of them as one's own to satisfy the requirements of a course" than any other act of dishonesty.

    Most cases of plagiarism that come before the Academic Honesty Board are blatant and deliberate. Poor time management, laziness, obsession with grades, lack of confidence in their own originality and opinions, are some of the reasons that students give for submitting the work of another without citation. None of these reasons justifies the theft of ideas or the attempted deception of faculty.

    Other cases of plagiarism arise from the students' confusion or ignorance as to when and how to properly cite material that is incorporated in a term paper or report. To remedy this problem, this "Pocket Keys for Writers" can serve as a safe harbor on the often stormy seas of research and writing. The section on plagiarism describes in plain language the basic rules relating to the form and manner of citation.

    A university, as with all other institutions of learning, cannot carry out its mission of producing educated people unless it rests on the foundation of academic integrity. Both in class and outside of class, truth, and its partner, trust, must be the basis of the relationship between and among students and faculty.

    The Academic Honesty Board hopes that this book will help you to succeed in college in an honest and honorable way.

Very truly yours,

Dr. William J. McDevitt, Chair
Academic Honesty Board

ACADEMIC HONESTY POLICY

The University exists primarily to sustain the pursuit of knowledge. Learning, to have true value, must be linked to a sense of honesty and integrity. It is the responsibility of every person in the academic community—faculty members, students, administrators—to ensure that dishonesty is not tolerated. Personal and communal integrity have always been fundamental in Jesuit education, and a sense of honor must be kept alive in every activity at Saint Joseph's University.

In order to recognize the essential contribution of honor to University life, an official Academic Honesty Policy has been adopted. This policy addresses violations in two categories: acts of dishonesty in formal courses and acts of dishonesty outside those courses.

1. Acts of dishonesty in formal courses

In all courses, each student has the responsibility to submit work that is uniquely his or her own. All of this work must be done in accordance with established principles of academic integrity. Specific violations of this responsibility include, but are not limited to, the following:

a. cheating, copying, or the offering or receiving of unauthorized assistance or information in examinations, tests, quizzes, reports, assigned papers, or special assignments, as in computer programming, studio work, and the like;

b. the fabrication or falsification of data, results, or sources for papers or reports, as in laboratory reports;

c. any action which destroys or alters the work of another student;

d. the multiple submission of the same paper or report for assignments in more than one course without the prior written permission of each instructor;

e. plagiarism, the appropriation of information, ideas, or the language of other persons or writers and the submission of them as one's own to satisfy the requirements of a course. Plagiarism thus constitutes both theft and deceit. Compositions, term papers, or computer programs acquired, either in part or in whole, from commercial sources or from other students and submitted as one's own original work shall be considered plagiarism.

All students are directed to the standard manuals of style or reference guides for discussions of plagiarism and the means by which sources are legitimately acknowledged, cited, quoted, paraphrased, and footnoted—whether presented in an oral report or in writing.

2. Acts of dishonesty outside formal courses

Students have other academic responsibilities that may pertain to conduct outside formal coursework and which also fall under the jurisdiction of the University Academic Honesty Policy. Specific violations of such responsibilities include, but are not limited to, the following:

a. the misrepresentation of one's own or another's identity;

b. the alteration or falsification of official University records;

c. the unauthorized use of University academic facilities or equipment, including computer accounts and files;

d. the unauthorized recording, sale, or use of lectures and other instructional materials;

e. the unauthorized removal, mutilation, or deliberate concealment of materials in University libraries.

While the main purpose of the University Academic Honesty Policy is positive, to stress the importance of personal and communal integrity within an atmosphere of learning, the commission of any offense of academic dishonesty makes the violator subject to penalties determined to be justified by the University, according to the procedures which follow.

3. **Primary Responsibility**

Primary responsibility for investigating alleged infractions of the University Academic Honesty Policy under section 1, above, rests with the faculty member in whose course the infraction occurred. The faculty member also has the responsibility for determining the sanctions, specified below, for infractions under section 1. Similar primary responsibilities for infractions under section 2, above, normally rest with the Vice President for Academic Affairs or his or her designee, hereinafter referred to as the Vice President. Primary responsibility for investigating infractions filed as complaints under section 5, below, and for determining the sanctions also rests with the Vice President. Whenever an infraction is alleged, the faculty member or the Vice President shall summon the student to an interview.

4. **Interview**

   a. *Notice.* An attempt to notify the student by letter or phone must be made within 10 consecutive days of the discovery of the alleged infraction. An interview is to be held as soon as possible after the student is notified of the alleged infraction. However, cases in which the time frame cannot be met will not be dismissed for this reason alone.

   b. *Penalties*

      i. Under section 1, above: After a review of the evidence, if a student is found guilty of an infraction, depending on its severity, the faculty member must either record a grade of zero or failure for the examination or assignment, or record a grade of failure for the course. In cases of failure for the course, withdrawal from the course is not permitted; in cases of failure or the grade of zero for an assignment or examination, withdrawal from the course must have the written approval of the responsible faculty member.

      ii. Under section 2, above: After a review of the evidence, if a student is found guilty of an infraction (excepting those under section 2.e.), depending on its severity, the Vice President must either suspend or dismiss the student. If a student is found guilty under section 2.e., one or more of the following sanctions may be imposed: restitution, fine, suspension, or dismissal. In cases of suspension, no credits for courses taken during the suspension will be accepted towards graduation requirements.

   c. *Files.* In all cases where a student is found guilty, the names of the principals, the pertinent dates, and the nature of the offense must be communicated in writing to the Office of the Registrar to be maintained in a separate, confidential file. In cases of second offenses, the Director of the Office of the Registrar shall immediately notify the Chair of the Academic Honesty Board.

5. **Complaints**

Any member of the academic community may file with the Vice President a written complaint against a student alleging that an infraction has occurred. If, after prompt investigation, the Vice President finds that the complaint may be justified, the Vice President shall investigate further, hold an interview with the student, and also notify the instructor of the course involved.

6. **Academic Honesty Board**

   a. *Composition.* The Academic Honesty Board shall consist of seventeen members: a chair; eight faculty members, including two from each of the four divisions (business, humanities, social sciences, and natural sciences/math); and eight students, including two from each of the four constituencies (CA&S, HSB, University College, and Graduate Programs). All members, including the chair, shall be nominated by appropriate deans or student governments and appointed by the Vice President, with consideration given to anyone interested in serving on the Board. All members shall serve two-year terms which are renewable. In the event that the chair is temporarily unable to convene the board, he/she will designate one of the eight faculty members to act as chair until such time as the chair is again able to convene. Six Board members, including the Chair (or his/her designate) and at least one student representative, constitute a quorum in order to conduct business. Decisions of the Board shall be rendered by a simple majority of those present. The Chair (or his/her designate) shall vote only in the case of a tie.

   b. *Appeals and Referrals.* An accused student may appeal to the Board in order to contest a determination of guilt if he or she believes the decision to have been unsubstantiated or procedurally unfair. The responsible faculty member or the Vice President may refer a case to the Board if he or she believes because of the severity of the offense that the penalties specified under section 4.b., above, are inadequate. All appeals and referrals must state grounds and must be made in writing to the Chair within seven days after notification of the decision.

   c. *Hearings.* As soon as possible after the receipt of a written request for an appeal or a referral, the Chair (or his/her designate) shall consult a minimum of four board members, including at least one student representative, to determine whether sufficient grounds exist for conducting a formal hearing. For cases in which it is decided that there are not sufficient grounds for appeal, a letter explaining the basis for that decision shall be written and mailed to the student who made the appeal. Upon notification of a second offense, the Board must hold a hearing to decide what further action should be taken. Written notice of a formal hearing must be provided to the parties involved, normally seven days before the hearing. Present at the hearing may be the following: the accused student, the accusing person, any witnesses or advisor from the academic community called by the student or the accuser, anyone called by the Board. The decision of the Board shall be communicated in writing by the Chair to the accused student and to the responsible faculty member or the Vice President, as defined under section 3, above, usually within seven days after the hearing.

   d. *Penalties.* If the Board finds a student guilty, it shall do one or more of the following: allow the original decision to stand; suspend the student for a specified period of time; dismiss the student from the University; or impose some other penalty which the Board deems more suitable. However, the Board cannot lessen penalties imposed under section 4.b., above.

   e. *Files.* The Board shall retain a confidential file on each hearing specifying the names of the principals, the pertinent dates, the nature of the charge and its final disposition. At the end of each academic year the Chair shall submit a summary report on the proceedings of the Academic Honesty Board to the Vice President.

   Approved by University Council May 20, 1982

KEY TO THE BOOK

■ Writing Process/Working with Sources ■ Sentence-Level Issues

KEY COMPUTER AND ONLINE FEATURES

WRITING ONLINE
E-mail and listservs, 11
Academic writing, 11
Online résumés, 11
Web page design, 12

RESEARCH ONLINE
Keyword searching, 15
Web caution!, 16
Search engines, 17
Indexes and databases, 17
Web sites, 18
Evaluating Internet sources, 26

WRITING IN THE DISCIPLINES
Research sources in 24 subject areas: print and
    online, 18

**CITING AND DOCUMENTING
ELECTRONIC SOURCES**
Indicating the boundaries of an electronic citation
    with no page numbers, 35
MLA style, 43, 55
APA style, 71, 79
CBE style, 85
Chicago style, 90
ACW and *The Columbia Guide to Online Style*, 56

PUNCTUATION ONLINE
In URLs, 169
Underscoring, underlining, and italics, 169
Capitals and hyphens, 170
Asterisks, angle brackets, and abbreviations, 170

COMPUTER NOTES
Spelling and grammar checkers, 3
Recording search results, 27
Templates for recording sources, 27
No indentation for online works cited list, 46
Word processing and hyphenation, 168

Visit the *Pocket Keys* Web site at
http://www.hmco.com/college
(click on English, then on *Pocket Keys for Writers*)

FIVE WAYS TO USE
POCKET KEYS FOR WRITERS

Pocket Keys for Writers makes it easy for you to find information quickly. Here are five convenient ways to locate the information you need:

1. Color-Coded Pages
Red sections cover "whole paper" issues such as the writing process and working with sources.

Blue sections cover sentence-level concerns such as style, grammar, punctuation, and mechanics.

2. Contents
The Key to the Book (inside front cover) is a directory to the book's eight parts.

Detailed Tables of Contents (on the back of each part divider) allow you to scan easily for the exact topic you are seeking.

Complete Table of Contents (inside back cover) shows the book at a glance.

3. Indexes
The Main Index (p. 203) provides a complete alphabetical list of topics, terms, and words such as *it's* and *its, who* and *whom.*

Specialized Indexes for MLA (p. 38) and APA (p. 66) include detailed coverage of documenting electronic sources.

4. Lists
List of Key Computer and Online Features (p. i) details technology-related coverage in the book.

Key Points Boxes (see list on p. 218) give quick answers to quick questions.

Useful Sources in Twenty-four Subject Areas (p. 18) is a list of starting points for research across the curriculum.

Correction and Editing Marks (p. 219) shows common symbols, with cross-references to related coverage in the book.

5. Glossaries
Glossary of Usage (p. 184) clarifies the use of commonly confused words such as *affect/effect* and *lie/lay.*

Glossary of Grammatical Terms (p. 192) defines helpful terms and provides cross-references to related coverage in the book.

POCKET KEYS
FOR WRITERS

Custom Edition for
Saint Joseph's University

ANN RAIMES
Hunter College
City University of New York

HOUGHTON MIFFLIN COMPANY
Boston New York

Senior Sponsoring Editor: Suzanne Phelps Weir
Basic Book Editor: Martha Bustin
Associate Editor: Jennifer Roderick
Editorial Assistant: Tamara Jachimowicz
Senior Project Editor: Rosemary Winfield
Senior Production/Design Coordinator: Jill Haber
Senior Designer: Henry Rachlin
Manufacturing Manager: Florence Cadran
Senior Marketing Manager: Nancy Lyman

Custom Publishing Editor: Dan Luciano
Custom Publishing Production Manager: Kathleen McCourt
Project Coordinator: Kayla Whittet

Cover Designer: André Mora
Cover Image: Saint Joseph's University

Copyright © 2000 by Houghton Mifflin Company. 2002 Impression.
All rights reserved.

All rights reserved. No part of this publication may be reproduced in any
form whatsoever, by photograph or xerography or by any other means, by
broadcast or transmission, by translation into any kind of language, nor by
recording electronically or otherwise, without permission in writing from the
publisher, except by a reviewer, who may quote brief passages in critical articles and reviews.

Printed in the United States of America.

ISBN: 0-618-29468-6
N01633

3 4 5 6 7 8 9 – CCI – 04 03

 Houghton Mifflin
                    Custom Publishing

222 Berkeley Street • Boston, MA 02116

Address all correspondence and order information to the above address.

Part 1
The Writing Process

1

Part 1   The Writing Process

1 Working through the Process

Engaging in the writing process means engaging in a variety of activities: identifying your purpose, audience, and topic; generating ideas; gathering information; establishing a thesis; organizing ideas; drafting; revising; editing; and proofreading. While virtually no one who is faced with a writing task marches neatly through a series of distinct steps, you will want to plan your time to accommodate the process. The most important features of the writing process are these:

> The process is not linear.
>
> It is a messy adventure; it is not done according to a formula.
>
> Very few writers achieve perfection on the first draft.
>
> Writing is a process of discovery, so it can be exciting.

Nonlinear as this process may be, it is helpful to keep in mind that generating ideas, planning, drafting, and revising are all important aspects of that process.

1. Establish clearly what the assigned task is and what you need to do to do it well. Ask for clarification where necessary. Pay attention to requirements of length, format, coverage, and tone.

2. Decide on your purpose for writing: Do you want to explain an idea, provide information, describe, tell a story, record your own experience, assess cause and effect, give a definition, argue for a point of view, or persuade your reader to take action?

2

3. Determine who will read what you write and what your readers will know, expect, and value. Regard a college instructor as a stand-in for a larger audience of general readers who do not know everything there is to know about your topic.

Readers of languages other than English may expect and appreciate obliqueness, ornate language, and digressions. Readers of English generally value simplicity and directness. ■

4. To find a topic or explore an assigned topic, generate ideas through reading, discussion, brainstorming, freewriting, outlining—any way you can.

5. Establish your approach to the topic and formulate a working thesis (**2a**).

6. If necessary, consult sources and record all source information (**4–6**).

7. Write a rough outline of the points you will cover to support your thesis (**2c**) and then write a draft.

8. Evaluate the draft by examining each paragraph: What main idea does each paragraph convey? Do details in the paragraph develop that idea? Does each paragraph's main point support the thesis of the essay or report? Does the information flow well, with no big jumps for the reader?

9. Revise as often as necessary, paying attention to content, organization, paragraph structure, transitions, and style (**14–18**). Work on giving your essay a good title, one that will make the reader want to read more. Check that your conclusion rounds off the essay, reinforces the thesis, and provides a frame for the essay, avoiding new points, apologies, and changes of opinion.

10. Edit for errors in grammar, sentence structure, spelling, mechanics, and punctuation (**19–39**).

Use the spelling checker in your word processing program, but remember that it will not find grammatical errors such as missing plural or -*ed* endings; nor will it find a misspelled word that is actually another word (*expect* for *except*, for example). A grammar checking program will analyze what could be fixed, tightened, or polished, but be aware that the capabilities of such programs are limited. ∎

11. Decide on presentation of the manuscript: title, format, margins, spacing, headings, lists, and visuals (3).

12. Proofread carefully to look for errors. Helpful techniques: Read aloud to a friend, with both of you looking at a copy of your manuscript; read your copy, covering up everything below the line you are checking so that your eye cannot run ahead; or ideally put your manuscript away for a day or two before you check it.

2 Stating a Thesis and Providing Support

Suppose someone were to ask you the question "What is the main idea you want to communicate to your reader in your piece of writing?" The sentence you would give in reply is your thesis. Your thesis tells your readers what point you are going to make about your topic, what stand you are going to take. It is not enough to say, "I am writing about bilingual education." The word *about* is far too general and wide-ranging. Instead your thesis must convey to your reader the *focus* of your essay, with, for example,

1. A strong, thought-provoking, or controversial statement

▶ **Bilingual education has not fulfilled its early promise.**

2. A call to action

▶ **All inner-city schools should set up bilingual programs.**

3. A question that will be answered in the essay

▶ **What can bilingual education accomplish for a child? It can lead to academic and personal development.**

4. A preview or reflection of the structure of the essay

▶ **Bilingual education suffers from two main problems: a shortage of trained teachers and a lack of parental involvement.**

2a A good thesis

You may find that you change your thesis as you do more reading and writing, but from the beginning do keep a working thesis in mind to focus your ideas.

 KEY POINTS

A Good Working Thesis

1. narrows your topic to a single main idea that you want to communicate;

2. asserts your position clearly and firmly in a sentence that makes a claim about a topic;

3. states not simply a fact but an opinion;

4. makes a generalization that can be supported by details, facts, and examples within the assigned limitations of time and space;

5. stimulates curiosity and interest in readers and prompts them to think, "Why do you say that?" and read on.

2b Organization of supporting points

Think of your essay as a structure of building blocks. At the top is the thesis, supported by your main pieces of evidence. Each piece of evidence, in turn, is supported by specific and concrete details. As you plan and begin your first draft, organize your ideas into a rough outline of numbered points, one that allows you to see the structure of your ideas and the specific examples that illustrate your ideas to your readers. Here is a student's preliminary outline of main points and specific examples:

Thesis: Shopping malls are damaging communities, social values, and business incentive.

1. Town centers are now deserted or are changing in character: Garden City, NY; Mall of America in Minneapolis; Atlanta, GA.

2. Teenagers who are attracted to the malls
   absorb the ethics of consumerism:
   Interviews with 5 teens; Deborah's story of
   how she spends every Saturday; <u>Time</u> magazine article.

3. Individual entrepreneurs and even department stores fail as malls and superstores
   take over: G. Fox in Hartford; Goldsmith's
   in Memphis; my neighborhood bookstore and
   hardware store.

3 Presenting Your Document: College, Career, and Online

Make your final copy as clear and attractive as possible. Poor presentation can seriously detract from your hard work in writing. A reader will feel attracted to a clean, well-typed manuscript, but not to pages of messy additions and changes.

3a College essay format

Follow these guidelines:

PAPER Use unlined 8½" × 11" white bond, not erasable or onionskin paper. Separate computer fanfold paper and remove the strips. Clip or staple the pages.

PRINT Always use dark black printing ink. Print in letter-quality type, not draft.

MARGINS Leave 1" all around; use a ragged right margin; do not justify.

SPACE BETWEEN LINES Double-space between lines.

SPACE AFTER A PERIOD Most style manuals suggest one space after a period or other punctuation. Your instructor may prefer two in the text of your essay.

TYPE FONT AND SIZE Use a standard type font (such as Times New Roman or Courier), not a font that looks like handwriting (such as *Jott*); select a regular size of 10 to 12 points.

PAGE NUMBER Use the "header" feature of a word processor to put a page number in the top right margin. Use arabic numerals with no period.

PARAGRAPHING Indent ½" (5 spaces) from left.

TITLE AND IDENTIFICATION Set this information on the first page or on a separate title page. See the following.

Title and identification on the first page See page 64 for a sample of the format recommended by the MLA for papers in the humanities.

Title and identification on a separate title page For MLA style, include a title page (unnumbered) only if your instructor requires it. Include the following, all double-spaced:

TITLE Center the title about one-third of the way down the page. Do not enclose the title in quotation marks, do not underline it, and do not use a period at the end.

NAME Center your name in the approximate middle of the page.

COURSE INFORMATION Place course and section, instructor, and date, each centered on a new line, either directly below your name or at the bottom of the title page.

For the social sciences (APA style), number the title page; include and center a running head, the title, your name, and your affiliation. See the sample title page on page 80. For a college course, your instructor may prefer that, in place of your college affiliation, you include your course number and the date on which you submit the paper.

3b Business writing

Business letters A good business letter is brief, polite, and to the point, conveying its main points clearly to the reader. It is written in relatively formal language and contains no errors. Single-space a letter; double-space between major sections. Do not justify the right margin to make all lines equal length as this causes gaps in spacing.

The sample cover letter for a résumé on page 9 uses a block format, with all parts aligned at the left.

Résumés   In a résumé, you need to show that your qualifications and experience make you suitable for the job you are applying for.

 KEY POINTS

Writing a Résumé

1. Use a laser printer, if possible, and print on standard-size paper of good quality, white or off-white.

2. Use headings to indicate the main sections.

3. Highlight section headings and important information with boldface, italics, bullets, indentation, or different fonts. Use a clear, simple design. Do not use elaborate fonts or design features.

4. Keep your résumé to one page, if possible. Do not include extraneous information to make your résumé longer.

5. Include information and experience relevant to the job you are applying for. Use reverse chronological order (begin with your most recent work experience and education).

6. Proofread your résumé several times and ask someone else to examine it carefully as well. Make sure there are no errors.

7. Accompany your résumé with a cover letter.

8. For posting a résumé online, see **3c**.

15 Maple Street
Iowa City, IA 52240 ←— Return address
April 5, 1999   and date
            ←— double space
Mr. M. Garcia
Personnel Director
Pluzynski Associates Inc. ←— name and
26 West 17th Street   inside address
New York, NY 10011
            ←— double space
Dear Mr. Garcia: ←— salutation with colon

I am interested in applying for the
position advertised in the New York
Times on Sunday, April 4, 1999. You
will find in me the "versatile and
energetic individual" you seek.

As you will see from the enclosed
résumé, I am about to graduate from
the University of Iowa with a major
in political science. My extracurric-
ular activities include counseling
foreign students, running a debating
society, and producing a video. My
experience with video and photography
would be useful in an advertising
setting.

I am available for an interview
during the last week of April or at
any other time convenient for you.
You can reach me at (319) 624-7918.

I am looking forward to hearing from
you and talking with you soon.
            ←— double space
Sincerely yours,

Kenny Liu

Kenny Liu

KENNY LIU
15 Maple Street
Iowa City, IA 52240
(319) 624-7918
E-mail KLiu@mercury.aol.com

POSITION DESIRED
- Public policy administration with city or state agency

EDUCATION
- University of Iowa, Iowa City, IA   1996–99
  Bachelor of Science Degree in Political Science May 1999
  Major average: 3.8
- Central Connecticut State University,   1995–96
  New Britain, CT
  Cumulative average: 3.4/4.0
- New Britain High School, New Britain, CT   1991–95
  Cumulative average: 89

WORK EXPERIENCE
- Cook, Paul Revere's Pizza, Iowa City, IA   1998–99
- Foreign student counselor, Peer   1997–99
  Counseling Office, University of Iowa
- Intern: New Britain Department of   Summer 1996
  Child Welfare

ACTIVITIES AND INTERESTS
- Chair, Debating Society, 1998–99
- Producer, promotional video on immigrants' use of social
  services in Iowa City, 1998
  Won campus prize for video production, 1998
- Poetry; photography; film and video production

SPECIAL SKILLS
- Word processing: 55 wpm
- Computer: Familiar with Microsoft Word, EXCEL
  (PC and Mac), World Wide Web, WIN98, HTML, and C
- Bilingual: Chinese (Cantonese) and English

REFERENCES
- Upon request and on file at Placement Office, University
  of Iowa, Iowa City, IA 52242

Further details can be found on my home page at
<http://www.polsci.uiowa.edu/~liu.html>.

3c Online writing

Online writing is developing its own conventions and re-quirements. For punctuation and mechanics online, see **33.**

E-mail and listserv postings Considering your busy readers is especially important with e-mail. Use the subject line to state your purpose clearly, and be brief. If you are replying to a posting, include only the parts of the original message that are relevant to your posting. Attach your name, e-mail address, and other information at the end; you can use a "signature file" command to create this text for every document you send. Even though e-mail is often in-formal, check your grammar, spelling, and punctuation be-fore you send a message that goes out to many people or to people you work with.

For more information on the conventions and etiquette (called "netiquette") involved in writing e-mail and listserv or newsgroup messages, consult <http://www.hmco.com/college>. Click on English and then on Writing Online.

Academic writing online Professors are increasingly asking students to submit papers electronically and posting them on course pages on the Web. Online you should pre-serve the same level of formality and standard forms of the language as you would for a paper copy. However, you will need to make several adjustments, such as the following:

- Use italics or electronic underscoring for titles and head-ings, not conventional underlining. Underlining online is used to signal a hypertext link.

  ▶ **Stephen King's *Misery*; Stephen King's _Misery_**

- Present your works cited without indentation for each entry. Instead, align each entry at the left and follow each entry with a line space.

- Include Web graphics, charts, and visuals to enhance your text wherever appropriate, but remember to ask for permission to reproduce the work of another.

Online résumés Posting your résumé on the Web is a good way to reach many prospective employers. You will, however, need to adapt your print résumé for online publication.

- Check out any prospective employer's Web site to find its emphasis and important keywords.
- Use nouns as résumé keywords to enable prospective employers to do effective keyword searches (use "educational programmer," for example, rather than "designed educational programs").
- Convert to ASCII (American Standard Code for Information Interchange) text.
- Use Courier or Times font, 10- or 12-point size; avoid bold and italic.
- Do not include vertical or horizontal lines or borders.
- Consult the Web site for the Division of Employment and Training in your state.
- For further advice and examples of online résumés, consult the Résumé Writing Center at <http://www.careermosaic.com>.

Designing your own Web page　For advice on designing a Web page and providing links to other Web sites, see "HTML Quick Start" at <http://www.projectcool.com> and also <http://www.glassdog.com>. Useful graphics are available from <http://www.andyart.com>. Netscape Composer also makes it easy to design a page without knowing HTML (Hypertext Markup Language) codes.

Part 2
Using Sources

13

Part 2   Using Sources

4 Searching for Sources

Writing often involves referring to what others have said about your topic—that is, it involves doing research and finding appropriate sources of information. Once you have found good sources, you need to record the information, synthesize it, integrate it into your own writing, and provide systematic citation. Allow plenty of time for this process and stay flexible. Research can involve false starts and frustrating dead ends, but flexibility and a curious attitude can make your research an exhilarating, gratifying journey of discovery.

4a Librarians

Do not feel daunted by the vast amount of information in libraries and museums and on the Internet. Your best resource is the reference librarian, trained to know what materials are available and how to locate them. Librarians can put you on track and direct you to valuable sources. Never be afraid to ask for their help in finding useful reference books, indexes, and databases (**4d**), as well as specialized sources.

4b Keyword searching

The first decision you have to make as you approach a catalog or database is whether to search by author, title, subject, or keyword. Keyword searching is the type most widely used for finding materials on a specific topic.

1. Find out from the database's or search engine's instructions on screen how to conduct a search. Many searches operate on the Boolean principle; that is, they use the "operators" *AND, OR,* and *AND NOT* in combination with keywords to define what you want the search to include and exclude. Imagine that you want to find out how music can affect intelligence. A search for "music AND intelligence" would find sources in the database that include both the word *music* and the word *intelligence*. A search for "music AND (intelligence OR learning)" would expand the search. You would find sources, in the database, that included both the word *music* and the word *intelligence* or the word *learning*. Some search engines let you use terms such as NEAR and ADJ (adjacent to) to find phrases close to each other in the searched text.

2. Use wildcard abbreviations (commonly * or ?) to truncate a word or to provide optional spellings. For example, *lab?r* will search for *labor* or *labour*; the truncation *music** will find instances of *music, musical, musicale, musician(s),* and *musicology*.

3. Require or prohibit a term. Many search engines allow you to use a symbol like + and no space before a term that must be included in the indexed document; a − symbol with no space following it prohibits a term: +"Civil War"−Gettysburg would direct the search engine to find Civil War but not Gettysburg.

4. Make terms into phrases. Generally you can use double quotes—"Martin Luther King, Jr."—or parentheses— (Martin Luther King, Jr.)—to surround a search term and group the words into a phrase. If you entered the search term *Martin Luther King, Jr.* without quotation marks or parentheses that signal a phrase, the computer would search for all instances of each word and could produce references to, among others, Martin Luther,

Steve Martin, Luther Vandross, Stephen King, and Roy Blount, Jr.

5. Be flexible. If your search results in no hits, try again with a different term or terms. Try variant spellings, too: *Chaikovsky, Tchaikovsky, Tschaikovsky.*

6. Use the results to help tailor your search. If your search produces only one useful source, look at the terms used in that one source and its subject headings and search again, using those terms. ■

4c Web sources: Caution!

Before you begin, check with your instructor about the role he or she wants Internet research to play in your writing project. In general, you should plan your research so that Web searching is a supplement to library research, not a replacement for it. Decide whether the time available to you will be spent more productively with traditional and online academic sources rather than with online discussion groups and individual promotional Web pages. Stay focused; once you begin Internet surfing, it is easy to be sidetracked.

4d Search engines, reference works, indexes, databases, and Web sites

To begin research in a subject area that is new to you, go first to general reference sources, indexes and databases, and, when appropriate, informational Web sites. These will give you a sense of the field and the issues. Many reference works and indexes are available online, some accessible on the Internet, some available only by subscription. Always check which general reference works and databases your library or your Internet Service Provider subscribes to. For specialized works in twenty-four subject areas, see **4e.**

- *Search engines for Internet searching* Many search engines are available to help you find the material you need on the Internet. Good ones to try are *AltaVista,* <http://www.altavista.digital.com>; *Excite,* <http://www.excite.com>; *Metacrawler,*<http://www.metacrawler.com>; and *HotBot,* <http://www.hotbot.com>. *Yahoo!*, <http://www.yahoo.com>, provides a subject directory.

- *Encyclopedias, both general and specialized by subject matter* Use general encyclopedias, in print or online, to check factual information and dates, consult the bibliographies listed, and do initial exploration of a topic. However, do not consider a general encyclopedia a major source for your research. Go beyond it to more specialized sources. Examples: *Encyclopaedia Britannica; Columbia Encyclopedia;* specialized works such as *Encyclopedia of Psychology*

- *Dictionaries, general and specialized* General dictionaries are useful for looking up word meanings, usage, etymology, and spelling. Specialized subject dictionaries, especially in the sciences and computer field, include explanations as well as definitions. Examples: *American Heritage Dictionary of the English Language;* specialized dictionaries such as *Dictionary of Literary Terms* and *Dictionary of Economics*

- *General reference works* In many fields, you will find survey works that present an overview of a field or collect relevant reviews. Examples: *Oxford Companion to African American Literature; Contemporary Literary Criticism; Oxford Companion to Art*

- *Bibliographies* Bibliographies list titles of books and articles on a specific subject. Examples: *Foreign Affairs Bibliography; MLA International Bibliography of Books and Articles on the Modern Languages and Literature*

- *Geographical reference sources* Consult maps, atlases, almanacs, and gazetteers when you need current information about population, boundaries, climate, products, and history. Examples: *Countries of the World; Columbia-Lippincott Gazetteer of the World*

- *Government documents* The Government Printing Office (GPO) provides numerous documents containing statistical information, useful for business, economics, and political science. Examples: *Statistical Abstract of the United States; Handbook of Labor Statistics; U.S. Census Bureau: Official Statistics,* <http://www.census.gov>; *Bureau of Labor Statistics,* <http://www.bls.gov>

- *Indexes and databases* Indexes, often on CD-ROM or online by library subscription, provide information about books and articles published in periodicals. You can find newspaper and journal articles published on a specific topic. Indexes often contain abstracts of articles and sometimes full texts. Online indexes and databases are best accessed by keyword searching (**4b**). Ask librarians about specialized indexes, too. Examples: *Reader's Guide to Periodical Literature; Infotrac; First Search; Lexis-Nexis; The New York Times on the Web*, <http://www.nytimes.com>; *ERIC* (education index); *PsycLIT* (psychology index)

- *Web sites for research in academic subject areas* Some Web sites contain vast amounts of information and useful links to other sites. Bookmark any sites you find useful. Examples: *The WWW Virtual Library* with basic sources in many academic disciplines, <http://vlib.org/Overview.html>; the University of Minnesota *Research Quickstart* site, with basic resources for research by subject, <http://research.lib.umn.edu>

4e Useful sources for research in twenty-four subject areas

This list of frequently used reference works in print, print and electronic indexes, and Web sites was compiled with the help of nineteen college librarians from seventeen colleges in thirteen states. These resources are particularly useful for giving you background information and for pointing you in the right direction for further research. Browse freely and remember to ask a librarian for advice if you have trouble finding a source or need a specific piece of information. Our Web site at <http://www.hmco.com/college> (click on *English* and *Keys*) contains hot links to the Web sites listed below.

Art and Architecture

Oxford Companion to Art
Lives of the Painters
Dictionary of Art
Encyclopedia of World Art
Arts and Humanities Citation Index
Bibliography of the History of Art
Art Abstracts (online and CD-ROM)
Art Index (online and CD-ROM)
Avery Index to Architectural Periodicals (online and CD-ROM)

The Getty Information Institute: <http://www.getty.com>
World Wide Arts Resources: <http://wwar.com>

Biology

Encyclopedia of the Biological Sciences
Encyclopedia of Bioethics
Encyclopedia of Human Biology
Henderson's Dictionary of Biological Terms
Biological and Agricultural Sciences Index (online and CD-ROM)
Biological Abstracts (online and CD-ROM)
Harvard University Department of Molecular and Cellular Biology: <http://mcb.harvard.edu/biolinks.html>
Zoological Record: Internet Resource Guide for Zoology (BIOSIS): <http://www.york.biosis.org/index.htm>
Biochemnet: <http://schmidel.com/bionet.cfm>

Business

International Encyclopedia of Business and Management
Hoover's Handbook of World Business
Encyclopedia of American Business History and Biography
Monthly Labor Review
Prentice-Hall Encyclopedic Dictionary of Business Terms
Ward's Business Directory of U.S. Private and Public Companies
ABI Inform (index online and CD-ROM)
Business Abstracts (online: full text)
Business Periodicals Index (online and CD-ROM)
Business Dateline (CD-ROM database of full-text articles from business journals)
Business and Industry (database with full texts of articles)
Bureau of Labor Statistics: <http://www.bls.gov>
International Business Resources on the WWW (Michigan State University): <http://ciber.bus.msu.edu>

Chemistry

Kirk-Othmer Encyclopedia of Chemical Technology
Ullman's Encyclopedia of Industrial Chemistry
Handbook of Chemistry and Physics
Beilstein Handbook of Organic Chemistry
Macmillan Encyclopedia of Chemistry
Encyclopedia of Chemical Terminology

Chemical Abstracts (online and CD-ROM, from the
   American Chemical Society)
ChemInfo (Chemical Information Sources): <http://
   www.indiana.edu/~cheminfo>
ChemistryResources: <http://www.chem.ucla.edu/
   chempointers.html>
NIST (National Institute of Standards and Technology)
   Webbook: <http://webbook.nist.gov> (physical
   properties for thousands of substances)
Chemicool Periodic Table: <http://www-tech.mit.edu/
   Chemicool>
American Chemical Society: <http://www.chemcenter
   .org>

Classics

Classical Scholarship: An Annotated Bibliography
Concise Oxford Companion to Classical Literature
Chronology of the Ancient World
DCB: Database of Classical Bibliography (CD-ROM)
Library of Congress Resources for Greek and Latin Classics:
   <http://lcweb.loc.gov/global/classics/classics.html>
The Perseus Project: <http://www.perseus.tufts.edu>

Communications and Media

*Webster's New World Dictionary of Media and
   Communications*
ABC-CLIO Companion to Media in America
International Encyclopedia of Communications
ComIndex (print and CD-ROM index of articles)
Mega Media-Links: <http://www.rtvf.nwu.edu/links>
WWW Virtual Library: Communication:
   <http//vlib.org/Communication.html>

Computer Science

Encyclopedia of Computer Science and Technology
Microcomputer Abstracts (online by subscription)
ACM Guide to Computing Literature (online and CD-ROM)
MIT Laboratory for Computer Science: <http://www.lcs
   .mit.edu>
Information Resources for Computer Science: <http://
   www.library.ucsb.edu/subj/computer.html>

WWW Virtual Library: Computing: <http://vlib.org/
Computing.html>

Economics

Dictionary of Economics
Prentice-Hall Encyclopedic Dictionary of Business Terms
Econlit (online by subscription)
PAIS (Public Affairs Information Service) database (online
and CD-ROM)
WebEc:WWW Virtual Library: Economics:
<http://www.helsinki.fi/WebEc>

Education

Dictionary of Education
International Encyclopedia of Education
Encyclopedia of Educational Research
Education Index (online and CD-ROM)
ERIC (Educational Resources Information Center):
supplies indexes such as *Current Index to Journals in
Education* and *Resources in Education*
National Center for Education Statistics: <http://nces.ed
.gov>

Engineering

McGraw-Hill Encyclopedia of Engineering
Compendex/Engineering Index (online by subscription)
Engineering Library at Cornell University: <http://www
.englib.cornell.edu>
WWW Virtual Library: Engineering: <http://vlib.org/
Engineering.html>

Ethnic Studies

The Historical and Cultural Atlas of African Americans
Oxford Companion to African American Literature
Encyclopedia of Asian History
Chicano Scholars and Writers
Native Web: <http://www.nativeweb.org>
African Studies at Penn: <http://www.sas.upenn.edu/
African_Studies/AS.html>
WWW Virtual Library: Migration and Ethnic Relations:
<http://www.ruu.nl/ercomer/wwwvl>

Geography

Encyclopedia of World Geography
Companion Encyclopedia of Geography
Geographical Abstracts (online and CD-ROM)
U.S. Census Bureau: U.S. Gazetteer: <http://
    www.census.gov/cgi-bin/gazetteer>

Geology

Glossary of Geology and Earth Sciences
Macmillan Encyclopedia of Earth Sciences
New Penguin Dictionary of Geology
Encyclopedia of Earth System Science
GeoRef (electronic index produced by American
    Geophysical Institute)
USGS (United States Geological Survey): <http://
    www.usgs.gov>
USGS Library: <http://www.usgs.gov/library>
AGI (American Geological Institute): <http://
    www.agiweb.org>

History

Encyclopedia of American History
Dictionary of Medieval History (Scribner)
Great Events from History series
Horus' History Links: <http://www.ucr.edu/h-gig/
    horuslinks.html>
WWW Virtual Library: History: <http://history.cc.ukans
    .edu/history/WWW_history_main.html>
*ABC-CLIO: America: History and Life and Historical
    Abstracts:* <http://serials.abc-clio.com>

Linguistics

The Oxford Companion to the English Language
The Cambridge Encyclopedia of Language. Ed. David Crystal.
The Cambridge Encyclopedia of the English Language. Ed.
    David Crystal.
The Linguist List: <http://www.emich.edu/~linguist>
Languages and Linguistics (on CMU's English Server):
    <http://english-www.hss.cmu.edu/langs>

Literature

Oxford Companion to Contemporary Authors
Dictionary of Literary Biography
MLA International Bibiography of Books and Articles on the Modern Languages and Literature (online and CD-ROM)
Project Bartleby (complete texts of books no longer in copyright): <http://www.columbia.edu/acis/bartleby>
The English Server (Carnegie-Mellon University): <http://english-www.hss.cmu.edu> with many links to many texts

Mathematics and Statistics

HarperCollins Dictionary of Mathematics
Statistical Abstract of the United States (U.S. Government Printing Office)
Mathematical Reviews (print)
MathSciNet (index and abstracts of articles: <http://www.ams.org/mathscinet>
WWW Virtual Library: Statistics: <http://www.stat.ufl.edu/vlib/statistics.html>
AMS (American Mathematical Society): <http://www.ams.org>

Music

New Grove Dictionary of Music and Musicians
The New Oxford History of Music
The New Harvard Dictionary of Music
Baker's Biographical Dictionary of Musicians
Thematic Catalogues in Music: An Annotated Bibliography Including Printed, Manuscript, and In-Preparation Catalogues
International Index to Music Periodicals
The Music Index (CD-ROM)
RILM Abstracts of Musical Literature (online and CD-ROM)
WWW Virtual Library: Music: <http://www.vl-music.com>
WWW Virtual Library: Classical Music: <http://www.gprep.pvt.k12.md.us/classical/catalog.html>
Indiana University Worldwide Internet Music Resources: <http://www.music.indiana.edu/music_resources>

Philosophy

Oxford Companion to Philosophy
Cambridge Dictionary of Philosophy
Dictionary of Philosophy
Routledge History of Philosophy
Philosopher's Index (print, online, and CD-ROM):
   <http://www.d.umn.edu/lib/online/philosophers
   .html>
American Philosophical Association: <http://www.udel
   .edu/apa>
Philosophy in Cyberspace: <http.www-personal.monash.edu/
   au/~dey/phil>.

Physics

Encyclopedia of Physics
Macmillan Encyclopedia of Physics
Physics Abstracts (online and CD-ROM)
American Institute of Physics: <http://www.aip.org>
WWW Virtual Library: Physics: <http://
   vlib.org/Physics.html>

Political Science

Political Handbook of the World (Annual)
Congressional Quarterly Weekly Reports
American Statistics Index
U.S. Census Bureau: The Official Statistics <http://
   www.census.gov>
The White House <http://www.whitehouse.gov>
United Nations <http://www.un.org>
PAIS (Public Affairs Information Service) database (online
   and CD-ROM)

Psychology

Encyclopedia of Psychology
PsycLIT (CD-ROM abstracts)
PsycInfo (online abstracts)
The Social Psychology Network (Wesleyan University):
   <http://www.wesleyan.edu/spn>
American Psychological Association: <http://www.apa
   .org>

Religion

ALTA Religion Database
Anchor Bible Dictionary
Encylopedia of the American Religious Experience
New Interpreter's Bible
Encyclopedia of Religion (print and CD-ROM)
Religion Index (online and CD-ROM)
*The Wabash Center Guide to Internet Resources for Teaching
    and Learning in Theology and Religion:* <http://www
    .wabashcenter.wabash.edu/Internet/front.htm>
Comparative religion: <http://www.academicinfo.net/
    religindex.htm>

Sociology

Dictionary of the Social Sciences
Encyclopedia of Sociology
International Encyclopedia of the Social Sciences
Social Sciences Index
Sociofile (online and CD-ROM abstracts)
Statistical Abstract of the United States: <http://www
    .census.gov>
Sociological Abstracts: <http://www.socabs.org>

5 Evaluating and Keeping Track of Sources

5a Evaluating books, articles, and Internet sources

Before you take detailed notes from any source, make sure it
will provide suitable information to help answer your research question. If your topic involves a serious academic
issue, your readers will expect your references to go beyond
popular magazines, newspapers, and Internet sources. Be
sure to diversify your sources.

Books

• Check the date of publication, notes about the author,
  table of contents, and index.

- Skim the preface, introduction, chapter headings, and summaries to get an idea of the information contained in the book and of its theoretical basis and perspective.
- Do not waste time taking detailed notes from an out-of-date book (unless your purpose is to discuss and critique its perspective) or a book that deals only tangentially with your topic.

Articles

- Check the date of publication.
- Evaluate the type of periodical the article appears in (popular or scholarly? See 6).
- Note any information given about the author or about the stated purpose of the publication: Is the article likely to contain an unbiased examination of any controversial issues?

Internet sources. The Internet is democratic. Anyone can "publish" anything on the Web. To distinguish between serious information and junk, do the following:

- Check the thoroughness of the document and the number of reliable print and Web sources it cites.
- Check the date of the material and when the information was last updated (in *Netscape,* check "Document Information").
- Scrutinize the author's credentials, if any are listed.
- Evaluate the purpose and objectivity of the sponsor of the site: What appears to be an article may, in fact, be an advertisement or propaganda.
- Beware of slick Web sites with no named author.
- Use the domain names in URLs to assess the quality of the information: *.edu* (education) and *.gov* (government) pages are more likely to include substantial information than a private individual's home page or a listserv posting.

    Useful information on evaluating Internet sources is available at a Widener University (Chester, PA) site, <http://www.science.widener.edu/~withers/webeval.htm>.

5b Keeping track of source information

Once you find good sources, whether in the library or on-line, you need to record what you find, in a form that will be useful when you write a draft.

 KEY POINTS

Checklist: When You Find a Good Source

1. Make a bibliography card (one for each source; use one side only) or fill out a bibliographical database on your computer. Record all the relevant information for each source you read and intend to use, including reference works. Record inclusive page numbers for all print sources.

2. Make copies of material you know you will use. Make sure to copy complete journal or magazine articles and the periodical's table of contents (which will provide date and volume number); with book chapters, copy the title page and copyright page of the book. You will need this information for your list of works cited.

3. Save material you find online by printing it out, e-mailing it to yourself, or saving it on a disk. Record complete document information (address, author, date posted or updated, if available), along with the date you access the material. Note a URL (Uniform Resource Locator) completely and exactly. Bookmark all the useful sites you visit so that you can easily find them again. ■

4. Read the copies you have made carefully. Annotate the copies with comments relating the source to your topic and thesis.

5. Take careful notes, relating what you read to your paper topic. Give each note a heading.

6. Distinguish exact quotations from summaries and paraphrases (7c), and record all exact page numbers, or paragraph numbers if given in electronic sources.

7. From our Web site (<http://www.hmco .com/college> click on English and on *Keys*), download or print and use the templates for recording information from books, articles, and Internet sources. ■

6 Recognizing a Scholarly Article

Learn to distinguish scholarly from nonscholarly articles.
Note the features of a scholarly article:

- It names the author and usually describes the author's credentials.
- It includes references to other sources, frequently in the form of a bibliography.
- It is substantial in length and substance.
- It appears in a journal that is published three or four times a year (not weekly).
- It appears in journals that do not include colorful advertisements for commercial products, gossip, or sensational stories. Scholarly articles published on the Internet are often sponsored by a university, professional journal, or research institute. Look for information about the author's other publications and research, bibliographies, source material used, and documentation.

When you read scholarly articles, scan any section headings, read the abstract and any section headed "Summary" or "Conclusions," and skim for the author's main idea to find out whether the article addresses your topic.

If you are working on a topic related to current events, you will probably consult newspapers and magazines as well as scholarly journals.

7 Citing Sources and Avoiding Plagiarism

Never get so involved in your notes and copies of sources that you try to include everything you have read. Make sure you leave plenty of time to read through all your notes, think about what you have read, connect with the material, form responses to it, and find connections among the facts and the ideas your sources offer. Anything that you summarize, refer to, or quote should support your thesis or illustrate a point you want to make—and the source should be cited.

7a Knowing what and when to cite

When you do refer to a source in your work, carefully cite and document—that is, systematically and thoroughly reveal the author, title, publisher, and date of your source. Provide such documentation as a service to your readers, so that they can locate the sources and read them for further information. Document sources so that there will be no question as to which words and ideas are yours and which words and ideas belong to other people.

Cite your sources and provide full documentation for all of the following:

1. all facts and statistics, unless they are common knowledge and are accessible in many sources;

2. quotations;

3. somebody else's ideas and opinions, even if you restate them in your own words in a summary (a brief exposition of the main ideas) or a paraphrase (see 7c on paraphrasing);

4. each sentence in a long paraphrase (if it is not clear that all the sentences paraphrase the same original source).

Citation is not necessary for facts regarded as common knowledge, such as the dates of the Civil War; facts available in many sources, such as authors' birth and death dates and chronological events; or allusions to folktales that have been handed down through the ages. If you are in doubt about whether a fact is common knowledge, cite your source.

7b Learning how to avoid plagiarism

If you present someone else's actual words or even ideas as if they were your own, either deliberately or inadvertently, you can be accused of plagiarism. The word *plagiarism* is derived from the Latin verb meaning "to kidnap." Kidnapping or stealing someone else's ideas and presenting them to readers as your own is regarded as a serious offense in Western academic culture and public life. Use the following guidelines:

• Do not include in your own essay a passage, an identifiable phrase, or an idea that appears in someone else's work without acknowledging and documenting your source.

• Do not use exactly the same sequence of ideas and organization of argument as your source.

- Always put an author's exact words inside quotation marks.
- Always cite the source of any summary or paraphrase (see **7c**).
- Do not just substitute synonyms for some words in a source. (See **7c** for acceptable and unacceptable paraphrases.)
- Do not use in your paper long sections that have been rewritten by a friend or a tutor.
- Never—but never—buy, find, or receive a paper that you turn in as your own work.

The Western view takes seriously the ownership of words and text. Copyright laws define and protect the boundaries of intellectual property. In some cultures, however, memorization and the use of classic texts in writing are common. And worldwide now, the ownership of language, texts, and ideas is currently being called into question by the democratic, interactive nature of the Internet. While the concept of plagiarism is not something universally agreed upon, in Western academic culture the ground rules listed in **7b** are very much in effect. ∎

7c Using paraphrase

A paraphrase is similar in length to the original material. It presents the details of the author's argument and logic, but *it does not use the author's exact words or sentence structure.* (See **7b** on avoiding plagiarism.) If you keep the source out of sight as you write a paraphrase, you will not be tempted to use any of the sentence patterns or phrases of the original. Even if you are careful to cite your source, your writing will still be regarded as plagiarized if your paraphrase resembles the original too closely in wording or sentence structure. You can use common words and expressions without quotation marks, but if you use longer or more unusual expressions from the source, always enclose them in quotation marks.

ORIGINAL SOURCE

We cannot legislate the language of the home, the street, the bar, the club, unless we are willing to set up a cadre of

language police who will ticket and arrest us if we speak
something other than English.

> —James C. Stalker, "Official English or English Only,"
> *English Journal 77* (Mar. 1988): 21.

The first paraphrase that follows cites the source accurately (in MLA style) but uses words and structures that are too close to the original. It therefore could be considered plagiarized.

PLAGIARIZED PARAPHRASE

As Stalker points out, we cannot pass legislation about the language we speak at home, on the street, in bars, or in restaurants, unless we also want to have a group of special police who will take us off to jail if they hear us not speaking English (21).

VALID PARAPHRASE

Stalker points out that in a democracy like the United States, it is not feasible to have laws against the use of a language and it certainly would not be possible to enforce such laws in homes and public places (21).

Even when you are careful to use your own words in a summary or paraphrase, you must still inform readers of the source of the information. In the paraphrase examples, note how the writer includes the name of the author and the page on which the original information appears.

8 Integrating Source Material

8a What, when, and how to quote

Deciding what and when to quote Quote sparingly and only when the original words express the exact point you want to make and express it succinctly and well. Ask yourself: Which point of mine does the quotation illustrate? Why am I considering quoting this particular passage rather than paraphrasing it? What do I need to tell my readers about the author of the quotation?

Quoting the exact words of the original   Any words you use from a source must be included in quotation marks and quoted exactly as they appear in the original, with the same punctuation marks and capital letters. Do not change pronouns or tenses to fit your own purpose, unless you enclose changes in brackets.

Omitting words in the middle of a quotation   If you omit as irrelevant to your purpose any words or passages from the middle of a quotation, use the ellipsis mark, three dots separated by spaces, within square brackets. If you omit the end of the source's sentence at the end of your own sentence, use three elipsis dots within brackets followed by the sentence period—four dots in all. Use three dots within brackets and a period if you omit a complete sentence (or more) when the omission is preceded and followed by complete sentences. See **29e.**

Adding or changing words   If you add any comments or explanations in your own words or if you change a word of the original to fit it grammatically into your sentence or to spell it correctly, enclose the added or changed material in square brackets (**29**).

The following example shows how a student integrates some exact words from the passage by Stalker on pp. 30–31 into her own writing, introduces the author of the quotation, indicates that she omits some words, and adds both a comment and a grammatical ending to make the quotation fit into her own sentence:

```
Educator James C. Stalker points out that
legislating against the use of any one partic-
ular language would mean "set[ting] up a cadre
of language police who will [. . .] arrest us
if we speak [and maybe also write] something
other than English" (21).
```

Quoting longer passages   If you quote more than three lines of poetry or four typed lines of prose, do not use quotation marks. Instead, indent the quotation one inch or ten spaces from the left margin in MLA style, or indent five spaces if you are using APA style. Double-space throughout. Do not indent from the right margin. Establish the context for a long quotation and name its author in your introductory statement, as in the following example.

```
Stalker also explains why in the United States
in particular all people must have the freedom
to use any language they choose:

            If any language group, Spanish or

            other, chooses to maintain its lan-

            guage, there is precious little that

            we can do about it, legally or oth-

            erwise, and still maintain that we

            are a free country. We cannot legis-

            late the language of the home, the

            street, the bar, the club, unless we

            are willing to set up a cadre of lan-

            guage police who will ticket and ar-

            rest us if we speak something other

            than English. (21)
```

NOTE: With a long indented quotation, the period goes before the parenthetical citation, not after it.

Avoiding a string of quotations   Use quotations, especially long ones, sparingly, and only when they help you make a good argument. Readers do not want a collection of passages from other writers; they could read the original works for that. Rather, they want your analysis of your sources and the conclusions you draw from your research. Quotations should not appear one after the other. If they do, your readers will wonder what purpose the quotations serve and will search for your voice in the paper.

8b Introducing cited material

Introduce quotations, summaries, and paraphrases and integrate them into the flow of your writing. They should not just pop up with no lead-in:

SOURCE NOT INTRODUCED AND INTEGRATED

Our ability to use whatever language we choose
is necessary in a free democracy. "We cannot
legislate the language of the home, the
street, the bar, the club, unless we are willing to set up a cadre of language police who
will ticket and arrest us if we speak
something other than English" (Stalker 21).

SOURCE INTRODUCED AND INTEGRATED

In an article critical of the English-only
movement, educator James C. Stalker points out
that we, as citizens of a free democratic
country, "cannot legislate the language of the
home, the street, the bar, the club, unless we
are willing to set up a cadre of language police who will ticket and arrest us if we speak
something other than English" (21).

Inserting a part of a quoted sentence into your own sentence
helps ensure that you introduce and integrate the quotation.

Naming the author (MLA style)   If you quote, paraphrase, or summarize a section of another work, introduce
the reference by providing in an introductory phrase the
author's full name (for the first reference to an author)
and a brief mention of his or her expertise or credentials.
For subsequent citations, the last name is sufficient. Then,
for a book or print article, give the page number in parentheses at the end of the quotation, followed by the sentence
period.

Varying the introductory phrase   Avoid always introducing a quotation with a form of the verb *say* or *write*.
Explore alternatives such as the following:

In fact, educational researcher James Stalker also
claims . . .

James Stalker, an educational researcher, makes the
following observation: . . .

Verbs like the following are often useful alternatives to *say* and *write: acknowledge, argue, assert, believe, claim, comment, contend, declare, deny, emphasize, insist, note, point out, propose, suggest.*

9 Indicating the Boundaries of a Citation

Naming an author or title in your text lets a reader know that you are citing ideas from a source. Then, citing a page number at the end of a summary or paraphrase lets the reader know when your citation ends. However, with one-page articles, and particularly with Internet sources, a page citation is not necessary or, with an online source, is not relevant, so this makes it harder to indicate the end of your statement about a source. You need to indicate clearly in your text where your summary or paraphrase ends and where your own comments take over. Convey the shift by making a comment about the source in a way that clearly reflects your own views. Use expressions such as *it follows that, this shows that, as a result, evidently, obviously,* or *clearly* to signal the shift to your reader.

UNCLEAR CITATION BOUNDARY

According to a Sony page on the Web, the company has decided to release <u>Mozart Makes You Smarter</u> as a cassette on the strength of research indicating that listening to Mozart improves IQ. The products show the ingenuity of commercial enterprise while taking the researchers' conclusions in new directions.

[Does only the first sentence refer to material on the Web page, or do both sentences? The boundaries are unclear.]

REVISED CITATION, WITH SOURCE BOUNDARY INDICATED

According to a Sony page on the Web, the company has decided to release <u>Mozart Makes You Smarter</u> as a cassette on the strength of research indicating that listening to Mozart improves IQ. Clearly, Sony's plan demonstrates the ingenuity of commercial enterprise, but it cannot reflect what the researchers intended when they published their conclusions.

Another way to indicate the end of your citation is to include the author's or authors' name(s) at the end of the citation.

UNCLEAR CITATION BOUNDARY

For people who hate shopping, Web shopping may be the perfect solution. Jerome and Taylor's exploration of "holiday hell" reminds us that we get more choice from online vendors than we do when we browse at our local mall because the online sellers, unlike mall owners, do not have to rent space to display their goods. In addition, one can buy almost anything online, from CDs, cassettes, and books to cars and real estate.

REVISED CITATION, WITH SOURCE BOUNDARY INDICATED

For people who hate shopping, Web shopping may be the perfect solution. An article exploring the "holiday hell" of shopping reminds us that we get more choice from online vendors than we do when we browse at our local mall because the online sellers, unlike mall owners, do not have to rent space to display their goods (Jerome and Taylor). In addition, one can buy almost anything online, from CDs, cassettes, and books to cars and real estate.

Part 3
Documenting Sources

10 MLA Style

At a Glance: Index of MLA Style Features

Author/Page In-Text Citations (10b), 41
A. One author introduced in your text, 41
B. Author not introduced in your text, 41
C. More than one author, 41
D. Author with more than one work cited, 42
E. Work in edited anthology, 42
F. Work cited indirectly in another source, 42
G. Reference to whole work, 42
H. Work only one page long, 43
I. No author named, 43
J. Electronic and Internet sources, 43

K. Other nonprint sources, 43
L. Organization or corporation as author, 44
M. Two authors with same name, 44
N. Multivolume work, 44
O. More than one work in citation, 44
P. Personal communication or interview, 45
Q. Classic literature and poetry, 45
R. Bible, 45

List of Works Cited (10c), 45
Books, 47
1. One author, 47
2. Two or more authors, 47
3. Book with editor, 48
4. Author and editor, 48

You need to document the sources of your information, not only in research papers but also in shorter essays in which you mention just a few books, articles, or other sources to illustrate a point or support your case.

MLA (Modern Language Association) style for the humanities is recommended in Joseph Gibaldi, *MLA Handbook for Writers of Research Papers,* 5th ed. (New York: MLA, 1999) and on the MLA Web site, <http://www.mla.org>.

Basic features of MLA style

 KEY POINTS

Two Basic Features of MLA Style

1. *In the text of your paper,* include the following information each time you cite a source:

   the last name(s) of the author (or authors);

   the page number(s) where the information is located in a print source. However, do not include the abbreviation "p." (or "pp.") or the word *page* (or *pages*). See **10b** for examples.

2. *At the end of your paper,* include a list, alphabetized by authors' last names, of all the sources you refer to in the paper. Begin the list on a new page and title it "Works Cited." See **10c.**

NOTE: Use endnotes (at the end of the paper) or footnotes (at the bottom of each page or at the end of each chapter) only for supplementary comments and information, not for regular source citations.[1] Number information notes consecutively in your text with a raised (superscript) numeral as in the previous sentence. Indent the first line of each numbered note. The following double-spaced endnote example corresponds to the superscript number above:

   [1] However, both MLA and The Chicago Manual of Style describe alternative systems of citation that do use footnotes or endnotes. See 13.

10b MLA author/page style for in-text citations

A. One author, introduced in your text   The first time you mention an author in your text, give his or her full name and, in the same sentence, a brief statement about credentials. (Thereafter, use the author's last name.) For a print source, at the end of your text sentence, give only the page number(s) in parentheses, followed by the sentence period. Cite inclusive page numbers as follows: 35–36; 257–58; 100–01; 305–06; 299–300. See **10c,** item 1, for the following work in a works cited list.

```
                   ┌── author ──┐
The sociologist Ruth Sidel's interviews
with young women provide examples of what
                    ┌───── quotation ─────┐ page number
Sidel sees as an "impossible dream" (19).
                                      period
```

When a quotation includes a question mark or an exclamation point, also include a period after the citation:

```
Mrs. Bridge wonders, "Is my daughter mine?"
(Connell 135).
```

B. Author not introduced in your text   If you do not mention the author while introducing the reference, include the author's last name in the parentheses before the page number, with no comma between them.

```
Many young women, from all races and classes,
have taken on the idea of the American Dream,
however difficult it might be for them to
achieve it (Sidel 19-20).
```

See **10c,** item 1, for this work in a works cited list.

C. More than one author   For a work with two or three authors, include all the names, either in your text sentence or in parentheses. See **10c,** item 2.

```
(Lakoff and Johnson 42)
(Hare, Moran, and Koepke 226-28)
```

For a work with four or more authors, use only the first author's name followed by "et al." (The Latin words *et alii* mean "and others.")

```
Researchers have established a link between
success at work and the pleasure derived from
community service (Bellah et al. 196-99).
```

D. Author with more than one work cited   Include the author and title of the work in your text sentence.

```
Alice Walker, in her book In Search of Our
Mothers' Gardens , describes learning about
Flannery O'Connor (43-59).
```

Alternatively, include in your parenthetical reference the author's last name, followed by a comma, an abbreviated form of the title, and the page number.

```
O'Connor's house still stands and is looked
after by a caretaker (Walker, In Search 57).
```

E. Work in an edited anthology   Cite the author of the included or reprinted work (not the editor of the anthology) and the page number in the anthology. See **10c**, items 5 and 6, for examples of the entry in a works cited list.

```
Des Pres asserts that "heroism is not neces-
sarily a romantic notion" (20).
```

F. Work cited indirectly in another source   Use "qtd. in" (for "quoted in") at the beginning of your parenthetical citation, followed by the last name of the author of the source in which you find the reference (the indirect source) and the page number. List the indirect source in your list of works cited. With the following example, Smith would be included in the list of works cited, not Britton.

```
The words we use simply appear, as James
Britton says, "at the point of utterance"
(qtd. in Smith 108).
```

G. Reference to the whole work and not to one specific page   Use the author's name alone.

```
Diaries tell us about people's everyday lives
and the worlds they create (Mallon).
```

H. Work only one page long If an article is only one page long, cite the author's name alone; include the page number in your works cited list (**10c**, item 22). See **9** on the importance of indicating where your citation ends, in the absence of a page reference.

I. No author named To refer to the work in your text sentence, give the complete title. Use a short title to refer to the work mentioned in parentheses.

According to The Far East and Australasia 1996 , the Buddhist calendar is the official calendar in Sri Lanka (38).

The Buddhist calendar is the official calendar in Sri Lanka (Far East 38).

J. Electronic and Internet sources Electronic database material and Internet sources, which appear on a screen, have no stable page numbers that apply across systems or when printed. If your source as it appears on the screen includes no text divisions, numbered pages, or numbered paragraphs, simply provide the author's name.

Science writer Stephen Hart describes how researchers Edward Taub and Thomas Ebert conclude that practicing music "remaps the brain."

With no page number to indicate the end of your citation, though, you must be careful to define where your citation ends and your own commentary takes over. See **9**.

If possible, locate material by the internal headings of the source (for example, introduction, chapter, section). Give paragraph numbers only if they are supplied in the source, abbreviated to "par." or "pars." and then include the total number of numbered paragraphs in your works cited list. (See **10c**, item 35.)

Kay also discusses powerless rulers and argues that the world of King Edward II is presented "as an admonitory negative example for the present" (par. 3).

K. Other nonprint sources For radio or TV programs, interviews, films, computer software, recordings, and other nonprint sources, include only the title or author (or, in some cases, the interviewer, interviewee, director, performer, or producer, and so on, corresponding to the first element of the information you provide in the entry in your list of works cited). (See **10c**, item 54.)

The director suggests that dying is not necessarily a depressing subject for a play (Jones).

L. Work produced by a business or corporation   Give the complete name of the organization in your text or a shortened form in parentheses.

The College Entrance Examination Board (CEEB) assures students that the test "reflects the type of work you will do when you get to college" (4).

Students are assured that the tasks on the test closely resemble the tasks they will have to perform in college (College Board 4).

M. Two authors with the same last name   Include each author's first initial, or the whole first name if the authors' initials are the same.

A writer can be seen as both "author" and "secretary" and the two roles can be seen as competitive (F. Smith 19).

N. Multivolume work   Indicate the volume number, followed by a colon, a space, and the page number. List the number of volumes in your works cited list. (See **10c**, item 11.)

Barr and Feigenbaum note that "the concept of translation from one language to another by machine is older than the computer itself" (1: 233).

O. More than one work in one citation   Include all the citations, separated with semicolons. Avoid making the list too long.

The links between a name and ancestry have occupied many writers and researchers (Waters 65; Antin 188).

P. Personal communication such as a letter, an interview, e-mail, or a conversation In your text, give the name of the person you communicated with. In your works cited list, list the type of communication after the author or title. (See **10c**, item 46.)

```
According to George Kane, Director of ZDNet
University, online courses are often less
expensive than courses in actual classrooms.
```

Q. Classic works of literature and poetry Include information so readers may locate material in whatever edition they are using.

FOR A NOVEL Give the chapter number as well as the page number in the edition you used: (104; ch. 3).

FOR A POEM Give line numbers, not page numbers: (lines 62–73). Subsequent line references can omit the word *lines*. Include up to three lines of poetry in your text, separated by a slash with a space on each side (/) (see **29d**). For four or more lines of poetry, begin on a new line and indent the whole passage ten spaces from the left, double-spaced and with no quotation marks.

FOR CLASSIC POEMS, SUCH AS THE *ILIAD* Give the book or part, followed by line numbers, not page numbers: (8.21–25).

FOR A VERSE PLAY Give act, scene, and line numbers, using arabic numerals: (`Tempest` 4.1.156–58).

R. The Bible Give book, chapter, and verse(s) in your text—Genesis 27.29—or abbreviate the book in a parenthetical citation (Gen. 27.29). Do not underline the title of a book in the Bible. Include an entry in your works cited list only if you do not use the King James Version as your source.

10c The MLA list of works cited

The references you make in your text to sources are very brief—usually only the author's last name and a page number—to allow the readers to continue reading without interruption. For complete information about the source, your readers can use your brief in-text citation as a guide to the full bibliographical reference in the list of works cited at the end of your paper.

KEY POINTS

What to Do in the MLA List of Works Cited

1. List only works you have actually cited in the text of your paper. Do not number the entries.

2. Begin the list on a new numbered page after the last page of the paper or any endnotes. Center the heading (Works Cited) without quotation marks, underlining, or a period.

3. List works alphabetically by author's last name. List works with no stated author by the first main word of each entry (**10c**, item 25).

4. Begin each entry with the author's name, last name first (or the corporate name or the title of the work if no author is stated). Omit titles ("Dr.") or degrees, but include a suffix like "Jr." or a Roman numeral, as in "Patterson, Peter, III." Give names of authors after the first in normal order.

5. If you include several works by one author, list them alphabetically by title and give the author's name only in the first entry. For all other entries, use three hyphens followed by a period; see the example on page 65.

6. Indent all lines of each entry, except the first, one-half inch (or five spaces). A word processor can provide these "hanging indents." Double-space throughout.

    For online documents, use no indentation at all. HTML does not support hanging indents well. Instead, follow each bibliographical entry with a line space. ■

7. Separate the main parts of each entry—author, title, publishing information—with a period, followed by one space.

8. Capitalize all words in titles of books and articles except *a, an, the,* coordinating conjunctions such as *and* and *but, to* in an infinitive, and prepositions (such as *in, to, for, with, without, against*) unless they begin or end the title or subtitle.

9. Underline the titles of books and the names of journals and magazines as in the examples in this section.

Use italics instead if your instructor approves and if your printer makes a clear distinction from regular type. Use italics for titles in all Web publications. See **33b**.

10. Give inclusive page numbers for articles and sections of books, but do not use "p." ("pp.") or the word *page* (or *pages*) before page numbers in any reference. For page citations over 100 and sharing the first number, use only the last two digits for the second number (for instance, 683–89, but 798–805). For an unpaginated work, write "n. pag."

▶ BOOKS

1. Book with one author On the title page of the book and on the copyright page, you will find the necessary information for an entry. Use the most recent copyright date and list only the first city on the title page. Use a shortened form of the publisher's name; usually one word is sufficient: *Houghton,* not Houghton Mifflin; *Basic,* not Basic Books. For university presses, use the abbreviations "U" and "P" with no periods.

```
                          first name
                 comma  /  ┌─period
   last name   /      /  /         ┌──────── title: underlined and capitalized ────────
   Sidel / Ruth.  On Her Own: Growing Up in the
   Indented
   ½ inch ──→ Shadow of the American Dream.  New York;
                                             period  │  colon
                      date                     place of publication
                 Penguin,  1990.—period
                     \  comma
                   publisher
```

2. Book with two or more authors Separate the names with commas. Reverse the order of only the first author's name.

Lakoff, George, and Mark Johnson. Metaphors
    We Live By. Chicago: U of Chicago P, 1980.

With four or more authors, either list all the names or use only the first author's name followed by "et al." (Latin for "and others").

Bellah, Robert N., et al. <u>Habits of the Heart:</u>
    <u>Individualism and Commitment in American</u>
    <u>Life</u>. Berkeley: U of California P, 1985.

3. Book with editor or editors   Include the abbreviation "ed." or "eds."

Gates, Henry Louis, Jr., ed. <u>Classic Slave</u>
    <u>Narratives</u>. New York: NAL, 1987.

With four or more editors, use the name of only the first, followed by a comma and "et al."

4. Author and editor   When an editor has prepared an author's work for publication, list the book under the author's name(s) if you cite the author's work. Then, in your listing, include the name(s) of the editor or editors after the title, introduced by "Ed." ("edited by") for one or more editors.

Bishop, Elizabeth. <u>One Art: Letters</u>. Ed.
    Robert Giroux. New York: Farrar, 1994.

If you cite a section written by the editor, such as a chapter introduction or a note, list the source under the name of the editor.

Giroux, Robert, ed. <u>One Art: Letters</u>. By
    Elizabeth Bishop. New York: Farrar, 1994.

5. One work in an anthology (original or reprinted)
For a work included in an anthology, first list the author and title of the included work. Follow this with the title of the anthology, the name of the editor(s), publication information (place, publisher, date) for the anthology, and then the pages in the anthology covered by the work you refer to.

Des Pres, Terrence. "Poetry and Politics." <u>The</u>
    <u>Writer in Our World</u>. Ed. Reginald
    Gibbons. Boston: Atlantic Monthly, 1986.
    17-29.

If the work in the anthology is a reprint of a previously published scholarly article, supply the complete information for both the original publication and the reprint in the anthology.

Raimes, Ann. "Out of the Woods: Emerging
      Traditions in the Teaching of Writing."
      TESOL Quarterly 25 (1991): 407-30. Rpt.
      in Writing in a Second Language. Ed.
      Bruce Leeds. New York: Longman, 1996.
      10-26.

6. *More than one work in an anthology, cross-referenced*   If you refer to more than one work from the same anthology, list the anthology separately, and list each essay with a cross-reference to the anthology.

Des Pres, Terrence. "Poetry and Politics."
      Gibbons 17-29.

Gibbons, Reginald, ed. The Writer in Our
      World. Boston: Atlantic Monthly, 1986.

Walcott, Derek. "A Colonial's-Eye View of
      America." Gibbons 73-77.

7. *Reference book*   For a well-known reference book, give only the edition number and the year of publication. When articles in an encyclopedia are arranged alphabetically, omit page numbers.

"Multiculturalism." Columbia Encyclopedia.
      5th ed. 1993.

8. *Book with no author named*   Put the title first. Do not consider the words *A, An,* and *The* in alphabetizing the entries. The following entry would be alphabetized under *C*.

The Chicago Manual of Style. 14th ed. Chicago:
      U of Chicago P, 1993.

9. *Book written by a business organization or corporation*   Alphabetize by the name of the corporate author.

If the publisher is the same as the author, include the name again as publisher.

College Entrance Examination Board.

  <u>Articulation and Achievement: Connecting</u>

  <u>Standards, Performance, and Assessment in</u>

  <u>Foreign Language</u> . New York: College

  Entrance Examination Board, 1996.

10. Translated book   After the title, include "Trans." followed by the name of the translator, not in inverted order.

Grass, Günter. <u>Novemberland: Selected Poems,</u>

  <u>1956-1993</u> . Trans. Michael Hamburger. San

  Diego: Harcourt, 1996.

11. Multivolume work   If you refer to more than one volume of a multivolume work, give the number of volumes ("vols.") after the title.

Barr, Avon, and Edward A. Feigenbaum. <u>The</u>

  <u>Handbook of Artificial Intelligence</u> .

  4 vols. Reading: Addison-Wesley, 1981-86.

If you refer to only one volume, limit the information in the entry to that one volume.

Richardson, John. <u>A Life of Picasso</u> . Vol. 1.

  New York: Random House, 1991.

12. Book in a series   Give the name of the series after the book title.

Connor, Ulla. <u>Contrastive Rhetoric: Cross-</u>

  <u>Cultural Aspects of Second Language</u>

  <u>Writing</u> . The Cambridge Applied

  Linguistics Series. New York: Cambridge

  UP, 1996.

13. Book published under a publisher's imprint
State the names of both the imprint (the publisher within a

larger publishing enterprise) and the larger publishing house, separated by a hyphen.

Krakauer, Jon. <u>Into the Wild</u>. New York:
   Anchor-Doubleday, 1997.

14. Foreword, preface, introduction, or afterword
List the name of the author of the book element cited, followed by the name of the element, with no quotation marks. Give the title of the work; then use *By* to introduce the name of the author(s) of the book (first name first). After the publication information, give inclusive page numbers for the book element cited.

Hemenway, Robert. Introduction. <u>Dust Tracks</u>
   <u>on a Road: An Autobiography</u>. By Zora
   Neale Hurston. Urbana: U of Illinois P,
   1984. ix-xxxix.

15. Republished book Give the original date of publication after the title and the reprint date at the end.

Walker, Alice. <u>The Color Purple</u>. 1982. New
   York: Pocket, 1985.

16. Book not in first edition Give edition number (*ed.*) after title.

Raimes, Ann. <u>Keys for Writers</u>. 2nd ed. Boston:
   Houghton, 1999.

17. Book title including a title Do not underline a book title included in the title you list. (However, if the title of a short work, such as a poem or short story, is included, enclose it in quotation marks.)

Hays, Kevin J., ed. <u>The Critical Response to</u>
   <u>Herman Melville's</u> Moby Dick. Westport:
   Greenwood, 1994.

18. Government publication If no author is named, begin the entry with the name of the federal, state, or local government, followed by the agency. "GPO" stands for "Government Printing Office."

```
United States. Department of Labor. Women's
     Bureau. Earnings Differences between Men
     and Women . Washington: GPO, 1993.
```

19. Dissertation For an unpublished dissertation, follow the title (in quotation marks) with "Diss." and the university and date.

```
Hidalgo, Stephen Paul. "Vietnam War Poetry:
     A Genre of Witness." Diss. U of Notre
     Dame, 1995.
```

Cite a published dissertation as you would a book, with place of publication, publisher, and date, but also include dissertation information after the title (for example, "Diss. U of California, 1998.").

If the dissertation is published by University Microfilms International (UMI), underline the title and include "Ann Arbor: UMI," the date, and the order number at the end of the entry.

```
Diaz-Greenberg, Rosario. The Emergence of
     Voice in Latino High School Students .
     Diss. U of San Francisco. 1996. Ann
     Arbor: UMI, 1996. 9611612.
```

If you cite an abstract published in *Dissertation Abstracts International*, give the relevant volume number and page number.

```
Hidalgo, Stephen Paul. "Vietnam War Poetry: A
     Genre of Witness." Diss. U of Notre Dame,
     1995. DAI 56 (1995): 0931A.
```

▶ ARTICLES

The conventions for listing articles differ according to the type of publication in which they appear: newspapers, popular magazines, or scholarly journals. For distinguishing scholarly journals from other periodicals, see 6. In all cases, omit from your citation any introductory *A, An,* or *The* in the name of a newspaper, magazine, or scholarly journal.

20. Article in a scholarly journal, continuously paged throughout volume For journal volumes with continuous pagination (for example, the first issue ends with page 174 and the next issue begins with page 175), give only the volume number and year.

```
                                    title of article,
last name       first name     ┌─── in quotation marks ───┐
   /               /
Hendrix, Lewellyn. "Gender Equality in
                  .
                period
```

```
┌──────────────────────────────────┐  ┌──────┐
Marriage: A Cross-Cultural View." Cross
   title of journal,
┌──── underlined ────┐  volume number
                              /
Cultural Research 31 (1997): 201-25.
                      |          \
                     year   inclusive page numbers
```

21. Article in a scholarly journal, paged by issue Include the issue number after the volume number, separated by a period.

```
Bell, John. "Puppets and Performing Objects in
     The Twentieth Century." Performing Arts
     Journal 56.2 (1997): 29-46.
```

22. Article in a magazine or newspaper Give the complete date (day, month, and year, in that order, with no commas between them) for a newspaper and weekly or biweekly magazine. For a monthly or bimonthly magazine, give only the month and year (item 23 example). In either case, do not include volume and issue numbers. If the article is on only one page, give that page number. If the article covers two or more consecutive pages, list inclusive page numbers after any section number.

```
Poniatowska, Elena. "No More Fiesta of
     Bullets." Nation 28 July 1997: 23-24.

Johnson, George. "Of Mice and Elephants: A
     Matter of Scale." New York Times 12 Jan.
     1999: F1.
```

23. Article that skips pages When an article does not appear on consecutive pages (the one by Greenwald begins

on page 94, runs to 105, and then skips to page 144), give
only the first page number followed by a plus sign.

```
Greenwald, Jeff. "Thinking Big." Wired Aug.
    1997: 94+.
```

24. *Review*   Begin with the name of the author and the
title of the review article, if these are available. After "Rev.
of" provide the title and author of the work reviewed and
publication information for the review.

```
Conover, Ted. "Flower Power." Rev. of The
    Orchid Thief, by Susan Orlean. New York
    Times Book Review 3 Jan. 1999: 9-10.
```

25. *Unsigned editorial or article*   Begin with the title.
For an editorial, include the word *Editorial* after the title. In
alphabetizing, ignore any initial *A, An,* or *The.*

```
"An Overdue Day in New Hampshire." Editorial.
    Boston Globe. 13 Jan. 1999: A18.
```

26. *Letter to the editor*   After the name of the author,
write "Letter" or "Reply to letter of . . . " with the name of
the writer of the original letter.

```
Hecht, Jeff. Letter. Boston Globe. 11 Jan.
    1999: A14.
```

27. *Abstract in an abstracts journal*   Provide exact information for the original work and add information about
your source for the abstract: the title of the abstract journal,
volume number, year, and item number or page number.
(For dissertation abstracts, see item 19.)

```
Van Dyke, Jan. "Gender and Success in the
    American Dance World." Women's Studies
    International Forum 19 (1996): 535-43.
    Studies on Women Abstracts 15 (1997):
    item 97W/081.
```

28. *Article on microform (microfilm and microfiche)*
Provide as much print publication information as is available along with the name of the microfilm or microfiche and
any identifying features.

Savage, David. "Indecency on Internet Faces
    High Court Test." <u>Los Angeles Times</u> 16
    Mar. 1997. <u>Newsbank: Law</u> (1997): fiche
    34, grid A6.

▶ CD-ROMS, DISKETTES, AND TAPES

Be sure to record the dates when the material was published
or updated electronically.

*29. Material from a CD-ROM or other portable
medium, regularly updated, with a print source* Begin
with the author's name, the title of the work, and whatever
print publication information is available. Then include the
name of the database (underlined), the type of medium (CD-
ROM, diskette, or magnetic tape), the name of the producer
or distributor, and the electronic publication date.

```
                                            print
┌── author ──┐      ┌── title of article ──┐  ┌─ source ─
Dowd, Maureen. "It Was Ever Thus." New York
    ┌────┐ ┌── date ──┐  page ┌─ name of database ─┐
    Times 18 Oct. 1998: 15. New York Times
                                     date of electronic
    ┌────┐  medium    ┌─ distributor ─┐  publication
    Ondisc. CD-ROM. UMI-ProQuest. 1998.
```

30. A single-issue, nonperiodical database publication
Cite material from a CD-ROM, diskette, or magnetic tape
published as a single edition (that is, with no regular updat-
ing) in the same way you cite a book, but after the title add the
medium of publication and any version or release number.

Keats, John. "To Autumn." <u>Columbia Granger's
    World of Poetry</u>. CD-ROM. Rel. 3.0. New
    York: Columbia UP, 1999.

31. Electronic source medium not known If you do
not know whether the material is on the library's hard drive
or on CD-ROM, use the word *Electronic* for the medium,
and give the name and sponsor of the network, followed by
your date of access.

"Renaissance." 1996. <u>Concise Columbia
    Electronic Encyclopedia</u>. Electronic.
    ColumbiaNet. Columbia U. 9 Jan. 1998.

▶ INTERNET SOURCES

The Web changes fast. For updated information on citing Internet sources, refer to the MLA Web site (<http://www.mla.org>) and the *Keys for Writers* site (<http://www.hmco.com/college>; click on English and then on *Keys*), where you will also find a template you can print or download to use to record the details of each source you find.

NOTE: If your instructor wants you to use Janice R. Walker and Todd Taylor's style for Internet citations, also known as ACW style (Alliance for Computers and Writing), consult *The Columbia Guide to Online Style* (New York: Columbia UP, 1998); also refer to <http://www.columbia.edu.cu.cup.cgos>.

 KEY POINTS

Citing Internet Sources

1. Give enough information in a citation so that readers can follow the same path you took and will find the exact same source. Because such searching requires exact details, record as much of the following information as you can find:

   - name of author, editor, or translator
   - title of work
   - any print publication information, including source and date, along with whatever information is available about page numbers in the print source: the range (5–15) or the number of pages (12pp) (see also item 5, following)
   - title of online site, such as the title of an online journal, a scholarly project, a database, a professional Web site, a personal site (all underlined), or the name of a discussion list or forum or subscription service (not underlined)
   - any version number or access number of material posted, or volume and issue number of an online journal
   - date when online material was posted or updated
   - name of the sponsor of the site, such as a library or university
   - date when you access the source

- complete electronic address (URL) or subscription service keywords

2. Give the date you access the material as the last date in your source reference, immediately before the URL or keywords. Two dates often appear next to each other in a source reference, as in items 36 and 37: The first tells when the work was posted or updated electronically; the second gives the date you find the material.

3. Treat FTP and telnet addresses in the same way as Web addresses.

4. Break a URL for a new line only after a slash. Never insert a hyphen in a Web address (a URL) and never split a protocol (e.g., http://) across lines. Always enclose a URL in angle brackets.

5. Include in your citation the page numbers for any print version of the source, but for the electronic version, include page or paragraph numbers of the on-screen version *only* if they are indicated on the screen. Usually they are not, and the page numbers of your print-out of the source will not necessarily correspond to other print-outs. When no page or paragraph information for the online version appears on the screen, include no page or paragraph numbers in your list of references. For citing unpaged online material in your text, see **10b**, item J. See also **9** on how to indicate where your citation ends.

6. Request permission to use any graphics or e-mail postings you include in your paper.

---

32. *Online book or part of book* Give whatever is available of the following: author, name of part, title of book, editor or translator (if applicable), print publication information, electronic publication information and date, date of access, and complete electronic address (URL).

```
       ┌─── author ───┐        ┌──── title of work ────────┐
Darwin, Charles. Origin of the Species.
           print publication
        ┌─────── information ───────┐      ┌ title of database ─
London: John Murray, 1859. Oxford Text
           date of electronic
        ┌──────────┐ ┌─ publication ─┐  ┌── name of sponsor of site ──
Archive. 4 Mar. 1993. Oxford University
```

```
                                    date of
                            ┌──── access ────┐
┌──────────────────────────┐          ┌──────────────
Computing Services.  9 Jan. 1999 <ftp://
      electronic address enclosed
────────── in angle brackets ──────────────────
ota.ox.ac.uk/pub/ota/public/english/

┌──────────────────────────┐
Darwin/origin.1783>.
```

33. *Article in a reference database* Include the title of the database, any version number, and the sponsor of the site.

"Bloomsbury group." <u>Britannica Online</u> . Vers.

    98.2 Apr. 1998. Encyclopaedia Britannica.

    7 Jan. 1999 <http://www.eb.com: 180>.

34. *Work obtained from an online subscription service* Libraries subscribe to large information services such as Infotrac, Ebsco Host, and Lexis-Nexis that provide abstracts and full texts of thousands of articles. Provide any print publication information, including the length (in pages) of the print version. If a URL is given, cite full details, including the name of the service, date of access, and the URL.

Lorch, Brian J., and Mark J. Smith. "Pedestrian

    Movement and the Downtown Enclosed

    Shopping Center." <u>Journal of the</u>

    <u>American Planning Association</u> 59.1

    (Winter 1993): 12pp. Infotrac SearchBank:

    Expanded Academic ASAP. 11 Jan. 1999

    <http://www.searchbank.com/searchbank>.

If the service provides a direct link without giving a URL, give the name of the subscription service, date of access, and any keywords used to access the source.

"Parthenon." <u>The Concise Columbia Electronic</u>

    <u>Encyclopedia</u>. 3rd ed. 1994. America

    Online. 9 Jan. 1999. Keywords: Reference/

    Encyclopedias/Columbia Concise.

If a library subscribes to a service but does not provide a URL, give the name of the library after the service and before the date of access.

35. Article in an online journal or newsletter Give the author, title of article, title of journal, volume and issue numbers, and date of issue. Include the total number of paragraphs only if paragraphs are numbered in the source, as they are for the example that follows. End with date of access and electronic address.

Kay, Dennis. "Marlowe, Edward II, and the Cult
    of Elizabeth." Early Modern Literary
    Studies 3.2 (Sept. 1997): 30 pars. 9 Jan.
    1999 <http://www.humanities.ualberta.ca/
    emls/03-2/kaymar1.html>.

36. Article in an online magazine

Benfey, Christopher. "Values, Shmalues: Don't
    Mistake Pieter de Hooch for a Stodgy
    Moralist." Slate 6 Jan. 1999. 7 Jan. 1999
    <http://www.slate.com/Art/99-01-06/
    Art.asp>.

37. Article in an online newspaper

Raebel, Joanna. "Personal Paths to Security."
    Los Angeles Times 5 Jan. 1999. 8 Jan.
    1999 <http://www.latimes.com/HOME/
    BUSINESS/WALLSTCA/t000001014.1.html>.

38. Review, editorial, abstract, or letter in an online publication After author and title, state the type of text: *Letter, Editorial, Abstract,* or *Rev. of . . . by. . . .* Continue with details of the electronic source.

39. Scholarly project

Perseus Project . Ed. Gregory Crane. 25 Nov.
    1997. Tufts U. 10 Jan. 1999 <http://
    www.perseus.tufts.edu>.

40. Professional site

MLA on the Web . 8 Jan. 1999. Modern Language
    Association of America. 12 Jan. 1999
    <http://www.mla.org>.

41. Linked site   If you connect to one site from another, include "Lkd." (linked from) after the details of the source you cite, followed by the title of the document you originally accessed (in italics or underlined), along with any additional details necessary for linking. Follow this with the date of access and the URL.

Hansen, Randall S. "Indispensable Writing

    Resources." 15 Oct. 1998. Lkd. <u>Keys for</u>

    <u>Writers</u> . 2 Jan. 1999 <http://

    www.hmco.com/hmco/college/english/

    raimes/frames/mlinkfrm.htm>.

42. Personal Web page   If the personal Web page has a title, supply it, underlined. Otherwise, use the designation *Home page*.

Kuechler, Manfred. 29 Nov. 1998. Home page. 8

    Jan. 1999 <http://maxweber.hunter.cuny.edu/

    socio/faculty/kuech.html>.

43. Online posting on a discussion list (listserv), bulletin board service (BBS), Usenet, or Hypernews   Give the author's name, title of document (as written in the subject line), the words *Online posting*, and the date of posting. Follow this with the name of the forum, date of access, and URL or e-mail address. For a Usenet news group, give the name of the group, beginning with the prefix *news:*.

Corso, Cristin. "Alternative Currents in South

    American Drawing." Online posting. 13

    Jan. 1998. LatinoLink Bulletin Board. 8

    Jan. 1999 <http://205.134.250.195>.

Wolff, Donald. "Comma Rules." Online posting.

    17 Nov. 1998. Writing Program

    Administration. 20 Nov. 1998

    <WPA-L @ASUVM.INRE.ASU.EDU>.

Hollmann, Annette C. "Re: Prestained Standards

    for Western Blotting." Online posting. 7

    Jan. 1999. 11 Jan. 1999

    <news:bionet .cellbiol>.

44. Forwarded online posting   To cite a forwarded document in an online posting, include author, title, and date, followed by *Fwd. by* and the name of the person forwarding the document. End with *Online posting,* the date of the forwarding, the name of the discussion group, date of access, and address of the discussion list.

```
Laurence, Pat. "WAC Resolution." 8 Jan. 1999.
    Fwd. by Carolyn Kirkpatrick. Online post-
    ing. 8 Jan. 1999. WID-TALK: A CUNY Inter-
    disciplinary Conversation about Writing.
    10 Jan. 1999 <WID-TALK@CUNYVM.CUNY.EDU>.
```

45. Synchronous communication When citing a source from a MUD (multiuser domain) or a MOO (multiuser domain, object-oriented), give the name of the person speaking or posting information, the type of event, title, date, forum, date of access, and telnet address or, preferably, a URL for archived material.

```
Delker, Natalie. Vertical file. "Cyborg
    Bibliography." Nov. 1997. LinguaMOO. 9
    Jan. 1998 <http://
    lingua.utdallas.edu:7000/4125>.
```

46. Personal e-mail message Describe the type of message after the title (if available) or after the author's name.

```
Kane, George. "Writing handbooks." E-mail to
    the author. 13 Jan. 1999.
```

47. Other electronic sources Identify online interviews, maps, charts, film clips, sound recordings, works of art, cartoons, and advertisements as you would sources that are not online (see items 49–57); then add electronic publication information, date of access, and the URL. For online transcripts of television and radio programs, include the word *Transcript* after the date of broadcast.

▶ OTHER SOURCES

48. Letter, personal communication, or interview Identify the type of communication (e.g., personal interview) after the author's name.

```
Rogan, Helen. Letter to the author. 3 Feb. 1999.

Gingold, Alfred. Telephone interview. 10 May
    1999.
```

Cite a published letter the same way as a work in an anthology. Include the page numbers for the letter.

Bishop, Elizabeth. "To Robert Lowell." 26 Nov.
     1951. One Art: Letters . Ed. Robert
     Giroux. New York: Farrar, 1994. 224-26.

49. Published or broadcast interview For print, radio, or TV interviews that have no title, include the word *Interview* after the name of the person interviewed, followed by the bibliographical information for the source.

Griffith, Melanie. Interview. Charlie Rose.
     PBS. WNET, New York. 14 Jan. 1999.

50. Map or chart Underline the title of the map or chart, and include the designation after the title.

Auvergne/Limousin . Map. Paris: Michelin, 1996.

51. Film or video List the title, director, performers, and other pertinent information. End with the name of the distributor and the year of distribution.

A Civil Action . Dir. Steven Zaillian. Perf.
     John Travolta and Robert Duvall.
     Touchstone Pictures and Paramount, 1998.

52. Television or radio program Give the title of the program; pertinent information about performers, writer, producer, moderator, or director; the network; and the local station and date of broadcast.

Mystery! "Cadfael 4: The Potter's Field."
     With Derek Jacobi. PBS. WNET, New York.
     21 Jan. 1999.

53. Sound recording List the composer or author, the title of the work, the names of the artists, the production company, and the date. If the medium is not a compact disc, indicate "Audiocassette," "Audiotape," or "LP" before the name of the production company.

Scarlatti, Domenico. Keyboard Sonatas . Andras
     Schiff, piano. London, 1989.

```
Walker, Alice. Interview with Kay Bonetti.
      Audiocassette. Columbia: American Audio
      Prose Library, 1981.
```

54. *Live performance* Give the title of the play, the author, pertinent information about the director and performers, the theater, the location, and the date of performance. If you are citing an individual's role in the work, begin your citation with the person's name.

```
Wit . By Margaret Edson. Dir. Derek Anson
      Jones. Perf. Kathleen Chalfant. Union
      Square Theater, New York. 12 Jan. 1999.

Jones, Derek Anson, dir. Wit . By Margaret
      Edson. Perf. Kathleen Chalfant. Union
      Square Theater, New York. 12 Jan. 1999.
```

55. *Work of art* List the name of the artist, the title of the work, and the museum or gallery and its location.

```
Johns, Jasper. Racing Thoughts . Whitney
      Museum of American Art, New York.
```

56. *Cartoon* Include the label *Cartoon.* Follow this with the usual information about the source and give the page number on which the cartoon appears.

```
Chast, Roz. "1998: A Look Back." Cartoon. New
      Yorker 7 and 14 Dec. 1998: 140-43.
```

57. *Advertisement* Give the name of the product or company, followed by the word *Advertisement* and publication information. If a page is not numbered, write "n. pag."

```
Viagra. Advertisement. Time 11 Jan. 1999: n.
      pag.
```

10d MLA paper format: sample pages

For general guidelines on presenting and formatting college papers, see **3a**. If your instructor requires a separate title page, see **3a** or ask for specific guidelines.

First page of essay

Fond 1

Stephanie Fond
Professor Ann Raimes
English 120-48
1 Dec. 1998

Shopping Malls: The New Downtowns?

Since the 1950s, shopping malls have been booming, even though not everyone loves them. In interviews, shoppers have described their local mall as "a kind of stamped out version of malls everywhere" (Glaberson B4), containing "hundreds of stores, many of which look exactly alike" (Herszenhorn). Still, the growth has been so extraordinary that it has caused Professor Kenneth Jackson of Columbia University to remark that shopping centers are now "the most common denominator of our national life, the best symbols of our abundance" ("All the World's" 1111). The result is that shopping malls are drawing people away from town centers and taking over many of the functions of downtown areas.

It is interesting to trace how this phenomenon has occurred. Jackson shows how city department stores such as the J. L. Hudson Company initiated the first experiments to capture the growing suburban retail markets (Crabgrass 103).

First page of works cited

Fond 10

Works Cited

Ellingwood, Ken. "Redemption for a Mall?"
Los Angeles Times 27 Jan. 1998: B1+.

Gillette, Howard. "The Evolution of the
Planned Shopping Center in Suburb
and City." Journal of the American
Planning Association 51 (1985):
449-60.

Glaberson, William. "The Heart of the
City Now Beats in the Mall."
New York Times 27 Mar. 1992: A1+.

Herszenhorn, David M. "A Retail State of
Mind." New York Times 16 Nov. 1997:
Sec 14: 1. New York Times·Ondisc.
CD-ROM. UMI-Proquest. 1997.

Jackson, Kenneth. Crabgrass Frontier.
New York: Oxford UP, 1985.

---. "All the World's a Mall: Reflections
on the Social and Economic
Consequences of the American
Shopping Center." American
Historical Review 101 (1996):
1111-21.

Moore, Janet, and Patrick Kennedy.
"Megamall's Success Stirs a Retail
Boom." Minneapolis Star Tribune 3
July 1997. America Online. 14 Nov.
1998. Keyword: Electric Library.

Moran, James B. The City That Was:
The Retail District. 1996. 10 Dec.
1998 <http://www.walshcol.edu/
~moran/detphot/detint.html>.

11 APA Style

This section gives details about the documentation style recommended for the social sciences by the *Publication Manual of the American Psychological Association,* 5th ed. (Washington, DC: Amer. Psychological Assn., 2001) and on the Web site for the APA *Publication Manual* (<http://www.apastyle.org>).

11a Basic features of APA style

 KEY POINTS

Two Basic Features of APA Style

1. *In the text of your paper,* include the following information each time you cite a source: the last name(s) of the author (or authors), and the year of publication.

2. *At the end of the paper,* include on a new numbered page a list entitled "References," double-spaced and arranged alphabetically by authors' last names, followed by initials of other names, the date in parentheses, and other bibliographical information. See **11c** for the information to include in the references list.

NOTE: Use endnotes only to amplify information in your text. Number notes consecutively with a superscript numeral; after the list of references, attach a separate page containing your numbered notes and headed "Footnotes." Include all important information in your text, not in footnotes. Use notes sparingly.

11b APA author/year style for in-text citations

A. A work with one author Mention the author's last name in your own sentence and include the year in parentheses directly after the author's name.

```
author      year
Wilson (1994) describes in detail his
fascination with insects.
```

(See **11c**, item 1, for this work as it would appear in a list of references.)

If you do not mention the name of the author in your sentence, include both the name and the year, separated by a comma, in parentheses.

```
The role of the Educational Testing Service
(ETS) in designing, evaluating, and promoting
the test has been criticized (Owen, 1985).
```

If you include a direct quotation, include in the parentheses the abbreviation "p." or "pp." followed by a space and the page number. All items within parentheses are separated by commas.

```
Memories are "built around a small collection
of dominating images" (Wilson, 1994, p. 5).
```

B. *A work with more than one author* For a work with two authors, name both, in the order in which their names appear on the work. Within parentheses use an ampersand (&) in place of *and*.

```
Harvard professors Slack and Porter (1980)
have pointed out that ETS cites research stud-
ies in a selective way.
```

```
It has been pointed out that ETS cites
research studies in a selective way (Slack &
Porter, 1980).
```

(See **11c**, item 13, for this work in a list of references.)
    For three to five authors or editors, identify all of them the first time you mention them. In later references, use the name of the first author followed by "et al." (for "and others") in place of the other names.

```
Jordan, Kaplan, Miller, Stiver, and Surrey
(1991) have examined the idea of self.
```

```
Increasingly, the self is viewed as connected
to other human beings (Jordan et al., 1991).
```

(See **11c**, item 2, for this work in a list of references.)
    For six or more authors, always use the name of the first author followed by "et al."

C. *An author with more than one work in one year* Identify each work with a lowercase letter after the date: (Zamel, 1997a, 1997b). Separate the dates with a comma. The reference list will contain the corresponding letters after the year of each work.

D. A work in an edited anthology Refer in your text to the author of the work itself, not to the editor of the anthology.

```
Seegmiller has provided an incisive analysis
of the relationship between pregnancy and cul-
ture (1993).
```

(See **11c**, item 4, for this work in a list of references.)

E. A work cited in a secondary (indirect) source Give the author or title of the original work preceded by "as cited in" to indicate that you are referring to a work mentioned in the work of another author. List the secondary source in your list of references. In the following example, *Smith* will appear in the list of references.

```
The words we use simply appear, as Britton
says, "at the point of utterance" (as cited in
Smith, 1982, p. 108).
```

F. A whole work or an idea in a work Use only an author and a year to refer to a complete work; for a paraphrase or a comment on an idea, a page number is not required but is recommended.

G. Author not named In your text, use the complete title if it is short (with capital letters for major words) or a few words for the title in parentheses, along with the year of publication.

```
According to The Far East and Australasia
1996 (1996),the Buddhist calendar is the of-
ficial calendar in Sri Lanka.
```

```
The Buddhist calendar is the official calendar
in Sri Lanka (Far East, 1996).
```

(See **11c**, item 5, for this work in a list of references.)

H. An electronic or Internet source Give the year of electronic publication or of the most recent update. If no year of publication is available, give the date on which you accessed the material. If you cite an e-mail message (personal, bulletin board, listserv discussion group, or Usenet group), cite it in your text as a personal communication (see item N), but do not include it in your list of references.

I. A nonprint source For a film, television or radio broadcast, recording, or other nonprint source, include in your citation the name of the originator or main contributor (such as the writer, interviewer, director, performer, or producer) or an abbreviated title of the work if the originator is not given, along with the year of publication: for example, (Morris, 1993). See **11c**, item 29, for this work as it would appear in a list of references.

J. A work by a business organization or corporation In the initial citation, use the full business name; in subsequent references, use an abbreviation if one exists.

```
One defender of the new test is the College
Entrance Examination Board (CEEB). The claim
is that "the SAT has been changed because edu-
cation has changed" (CEEB, 1993, p. 4).
```

(See **11c**, item 6, for this work in a list of references.)

K. A work by two authors with the same last name Use the authors' initials as well, even if the dates of publication differ.

```
F. Smith (1982) has described a writer as hav-
ing competitive roles: author and secretary.
```

L. A work with more than one volume Include in your citation the year of publication for the volume you are citing: (Barr & Feigenbaum, 1982). If you refer to more than one volume, give inclusive years for the volumes you cite: (Barr & Feigenbaum, 1981–1986). (See **11c**, item 8, for this work in a list of references.)

M. More than one source in the citation List the sources in alphabetical order, separated by semicolons. For works by the same author, list chronologically (earliest source first) or identified with *a, b,* and so on for works published in the same year.

```
Criticisms of large-scale educational testing
abound (Crouse & Trusheim, 1988; Hoffman, 1962;
Nairn, 1978, 1980; Raimes, 1990a, 1990b).
```

N. A personal communication, such as a conversation, a letter, e-mail, an electronic discussion group, or an interview Give the last name and initial(s) of the author of the communication and an exact date. Do not include a citation in your list of references.

```
According to Dr. C. S. Apstein, Boston
University School of Medicine, funding for
research in heart disease is diminishing (per-
sonal communication, January 7, 2002).
```

O. A classic work If the date of publication of a classic work is not known, use in your citation "n.d." for "no date." If you use a translation, give the year of the translation, preceded by "trans." You do not need a reference list entry for the Bible or ancient classic works. Just give information about book and line numbers in your text.

APA list of references

KEY POINTS

What to Do in the APA List of References

1. List only works you have cited (quoted, summarized, paraphrased, or commented on) in the text of your paper, not everything you have read.

2. Start the list on a new numbered page after the last page of text or notes. Center the heading "References," without quotation marks, not underlined, and with no period following it. Place any tables and charts after the "References" page.

3. Begin each entry with the author's name, last name first, followed by an initial or initials. Give any authors' names after the first in the same inverted form, separated by commas. Do not use "et al."

4. List the works alphabetically, by last name of primary authors. Do not number the entries. Arrange several works by the same author chronologically and give the author's name in each entry.

   Alphabetize by title an author's works published in the same year and distinguish with *a*, *b*, and so on after the date. *(continued)*

(continued)

5. Put the date in parentheses after the authors' names. For magazines and newspapers, do not abbreviate the names of months.

6. Use a period and one space to separate the main parts of each entry. Double-space throughout.

7. In titles of books and articles, capitalize only the first word of the title or subtitle and any proper nouns or adjectives. Italicize the title of a book and the period following it, but do not italicize or use quotation marks around the titles of articles.

8. For magazines and journals, italicize the publication name, volume number, and comma. Italicize the names of newspapers.

9. Give inclusive page numbers for articles and sections of books, using complete page spans ("251–259"). Use the abbreviation "p." (page) or "pp." (pages) only for newspaper articles and sections (such as chapters) of books.

10. Indent all lines except the first of each entry five spaces. Use no indents for Web publications, but add a space between entries.

▶ BOOKS

1. Book with one author You will find all the necessary information on the title page and the copyright page of the book. Use the most recent copyright date. Include city and state of publication or name of major city alone. Give the publisher's name in a shortened but intelligible form, including words like *Press* but omitting *Co.* or *Inc.*

```
last name    initials
      \  comma  /  periods
       \   |   /     \
        \  |  /       year in parentheses   title italicized
         \ | /           \      period      /         period
          \|/             \      |         /            |
Wilson, E. O. (1994). Naturalist.

⟷ Washington, DC: Island.
                |        /    |        \
           place of   colon publisher  final period
           publication
```

2. Book with two or more authors Reverse the order of all the names: last name first, followed by initials. Separate all names by commas, and use an ampersand (&) before the last name.

Jordan, J. V., Kaplan, A. G., Miller, J. B.,
    Stiver, I. P., & Surrey, J. L. (1991).
    Women's growth in connection: Writings
    from the Stone Center. New York:
    Guilford Press.

3. Edited book Use "Ed." or "Eds." for one or more editors.

Denmark, F., & Paludi, M. (Eds.). (1993).
    Psychology of women: A handbook of issues
    and theories. Westport, CT: Greenwood.

4. Work in an anthology or reference book List the author, date of publication of the edited book, and the title of the work first. Follow this with the names of the editors of the book (not inverted), the title of the book, and the page numbers (preceded by "pp.") of the chapter in parentheses. End with the place of publication and the publisher. If you cite more than one article in an edited work, include full bibliographical details in each entry.

Seegmiller, B. (1993). Pregnancy. In F.
    Denmark & M. Paludi (Eds.), *Psychology of*
    women: A handbook of issues and theories
    (pp. 437-474). Westport, CT: Greenwood.

For a well-known reference book with unsigned alphabetical entries, give only the edition number and year of publication. When articles are arranged alphabetically in an encyclopedia, omit page numbers.

Multiculturalism. (2000). In *Columbia*
    Encyclopedia (6th ed.).

5. Book with no author named Put the title first. Ignore *A, An,* and *The* when alphabetizing.

The Far East and Australasia 1996. (1996).
    London: Europa.

6. Book written by a business organization or corporation Give the name of the corporate author first. If the publisher is the same as the author, write "Author" for the name of the publisher.

College Entrance Examination Board. (1999).

    Index of majors and graduate degrees

    2000. New York: Author.

7. Translated book Give the initials and last name of the translator, followed by a comma and "Trans."

Jung, C. G. (1960). *On the nature of the psyche*

    (R. F. C. Hull, Trans.). Princeton, NJ:

    Princeton University Press.

8. Multivolume work Give the number of volumes after the title. The date should include the range of years of publication, wherever appropriate.

Barr, A., & Feigenbaum, E. A. (1981–1986).

    The handbook of artificial intelligence

    (Vols. 1–4). Reading, MA: Addison-Wesley.

9. Foreword, preface, introduction, or afterword List the name of the author of the book element cited. Follow the date with the name of the element, the title of the book, and the page number(s) for the element.

Weiss, B. (Ed.). (1982). Introduction.

    American education and the European

    immigrant 1840-1940 (pp. xi-xxviii).

    Urbana, IL: University of Illinois Press.

10. Republished book After the author's name, give the most recent date of publication. At the end, in parentheses add "Original work published" and the date. In your text citation, give both dates: (Smith, 1793/1976).

Smith, A. (1976). *An inquiry into the nature*

    and causes of the wealth of nations.

    Chicago: University of Chicago Press.

    (Original work published 1793)

11. *Technical report* Give the report number ("Rep. No.") after the title.

```
Breland, H. M., & Jones, R. J. (1982).
    Perceptions of writing skill (Rep. No.
    82-4). New York: College Entrance
    Examination Board.
```

12. *Dissertation or abstract* For a manuscript source, give the university and year of the dissertation and the volume and page numbers of *DAI.*

```
Salzberg, A. (1992). Behavioral phenomena of
    homeless women in San Diego county
    (Doctoral dissertation, United States
    International University, 1992).
    Dissertation Abstracts International, 52,
    4482.
```

For a microfilm source, also include in parentheses at the end of the entry the university microfilm number. For a CD-ROM source, include "CD-ROM" after the title; then name the electronic source of the information and the access number. (See **11c**, item 21.)

▶ ARTICLES

13. *Article in a scholarly journal, continuously paged throughout volume* Give only the volume number and year for journals that number pages sequentially for each issue in a volume. Italicize the volume number and the following comma as well as the title of the journal. Do not use "p." or "pp." with page numbers. Do not abbreviate months. For the title of an article, use capital letters only for the first word of a title or subtitle and for proper nouns. See **6** on recognizing scholarly journals.

```
Slack, W. D., & Porter, D. (1980). The SAT:
```
                                    journal title, volume number
     – no quotation marks around title ⌐   ⌐— & commas italicized ——
```
    A critical appraisal. Harvard Educational
```
                    no "p." or "pp."
    ————————⌐   ⌐————————before page numbers
```
    Review, 50, 154-175.
```

14. Article in a scholarly journal, paged by issue Include the issue number in parentheses (not in italics) immediately following the volume number.

Ginat, R. (2000). The Soviet Union and the
    Syrian Ba'th regime: From hesitation to
    rapprochement. *Middle Eastern Studies*,
    36(2), 150-171.
     issue number not in italics

15. Article in a magazine Include the year and month or month and date of publication in parentheses. Italicize the magazine title, the volume number, and the comma that follows; then give the page number or numbers.

           year,
      ⌐— month, date —⌐
Naughton, K. (2000, July 10). Bring on the junk
    food. *Newsweek*, *136*, 44.
             volume number included and italicized

16. Article in a newspaper Include the month and date of publication after the year. Give the section letter or number before the page, where applicable. Use "p." and "pp." with page numbers. Do not omit *The* from the title of a newspaper.

Navarro, M. (2000, July 13). Bricks, mortar,
    and coalition building. *The New York*
    Times, pp. A1, A16-17.

17. Article that skips pages Give all the page numbers, separated by commas.

Specter, M. (2001, November 26). The phone
    guy. *The New Yorker*, pp. 62, 67-72.

18. Review After the title, add in brackets a description of the work reviewed and identify the medium: book, film, or video, for example.

Weatherall, D. J. (2000, June 18). No panaceas
    [Review of the book *The elusive magic*
    bullet: The search for the perfect drug].
    The Times Literary Supplement, p. 32.

19. Editorial or work with no author named For a work with no author named, begin the listing with the title; for an editorial, add the word "Editorial" in brackets.

```
Air-traveler abuse [Editorial]. (2000, July
     25). The Washington Post, p. A22.
```

20. Letter to the editor Write "Letter to the editor" in brackets after the date or the title of the letter, if it has one.

```
Goldstone, R. J. (2000, July 7). [Letter to the
     editor]. The Wall Street Journal, p. A13.
```

▶ Electronic and Internet sources

Provide enough information to enable your reader to find the material you refer to. See examples of documentation at <http://www.apa.org>.

Include in your citation whatever information is available of the following: author; date of work; title of work; print publication information (items 1–20, above); identification of type of source, in square brackets (for example, [letter to the editor]); and name of information service and document number for an online service, or "Retrieved (date) ... from followed by the exact electronic address (the URL), with no final period. Include also any log-in instructions.

21. Universities and libraries subscribe to large searchable databases, such as *InfoTrac, EBSCO, ERIC, Lexis-Nexis,* and *WilsonWeb,* providing access to abstracts and full-text articles. In addition to print information, provide the name of the database and the date of retrieval and the item number if it is provided

```
Goldstein, B. S. C., & Harris, K. C. (2000).
     Consultant practices in two heterogeneous
     Latino schools. The School Psychology
     Review, 29, 368-377. Retrieved March 9,
     2002, from WilsonWeb Education Full Text
     database (0279-6015).
```

For works retrieved from generally available Web databases, such as government or newspaper databases, provide the URL.

22. *Online abstract*

Zadra, A., & Donderi, D. C. (2000, May).

　　Nightmares and bad dreams: Their

　　prevalence and relationship to

　　well-being. *Journal of Abnormal*

　　Psychology, 109, 273-281. Abstract

　　retrieved July 17, 2000, from http://

　　www.apa.org/journals/abn/500ab.html#11

23. *Online article with a print source* Give the author, date of print source, title, published source and page numbers (if available), date of retrieval, and complete retrieval information.

Jones, C. C., & Meredith, W. (2000, June).

　　Developmental paths of psychological

　　health from early adolescence to later

　　adulthood. *Psychology and Aging, 15*,

　　351-360. Retrieved July 17, 2000, from

　　http://www.apa.org/journals/pag/

　　pag152351.html

24. *Article in an online journal with no print source* Give paragraph length of the article in square brackets.

Holtzworth-Munroe, A. (2000, June). Domestic

　　violence: Combining scientific inquiry and

　　advocacy [10 paragraphs]. *Prevention &*

　　Treatment, 3. Retrieved July 18, 2000,

　　from http://journals.apa.org/prevention/

　　volume3/pre0030022c.html

25. *E-mail, contributions to discussion lists, and Usenet groups* Cite all e-mail documents as personal communications in the text of your paper. See **11b**, item N, for an example. Include a discussion list posting in your list of references only if it is archived.

Peckham, I. (2000, May 1). Class origins.

　　Message posted to WPA-L eletronic

　　mailing list, archived at

　　http://lists.asu.edu

26. *Computer software*

SnagIt [Computer software]. (2001). E.
    Lansing, MI: TechSmith.

▶ OTHER SOURCES

27. *Personal communication (letter, telephone conversation, or interview)* Cite a personal communication only in your text. (See **11b**, item N.) Do not include it in your list of references.

28. *Film, recording, or video* State the medium in brackets after the title.

Morris, E. (Director). (1993). *A brief*
    history of time [Video]. Hollywood:
    Paramount.

29. *Television or radio program*

Kayser, W. (Moderator). (1994).
    A glorious accident. New York: WNET.

11d APA paper format: sample pages

The following sample pages are from a paper written for a college course in experimental psychology. They follow APA style guidelines. Check with your instructor as he or she may want to modify the format, especially for the title page. APA style uses headings to indicate sections in the paper. Main headings are centered, and subheadings are flush left and italicized. Main headings include *Method, Results, Discussion,* and *Conclusions.*

Title page

Time Estimation 1

Running head: TIME ESTIMATION

Occupied and Unoccupied Time
and Their Effects on Time Estimation
Clay Guthrie

Hunter College of the City University
of New York

Abstract

Time Estimation 2

Abstract

Time estimation was studied as a
function of two variables: occupied time
and unoccupied time. Participants were
told in advance they would be required to
estimate four intervals of time. These
intervals were of equal duration. During
the unoccupied intervals, participants
sat at rest. For the occupied intervals,
they performed a word puzzle. A test was
run on the combined data, and the results
support the hypothesis that occupied
time is perceived as shorter than unoccupied time. The current findings support
the findings of Gulliksen (1927) and Brown
(1985) that time perception depends primarily on the way in which the individual
is occupied.

First page of paper

Occupied and Unoccupied Time and
Their Effects on Time Estimation
It is common knowledge that one's
perception of time may vary depending on
the activity one is engaged in. A person
may be engrossed in conversation, only to
realize that what feels like only a few
minutes is actually more than an hour.
In contrast, waiting for a tardy acquain-
tance may make every minute seem like an
hour.

Experiments on time perception have
supported these impressions, using a variety of tasks: anagrams and word games
(Curton & Lordahl, 1974; DeWolfe & Duncan,
1959; Gulliksen, 1927; McClain, 1983),
mathematical tasks (Gulliksen, 1927), and
the Stroop Task, involving color-word in-
congruities (Marshall & Wilsoncroft,
1989). These tasks vary in their degrees
of difficulty or "levels of behavior."

Axel (1924) used the phrase "levels
of behavior" to refer to every character-
istic of a task (such as difficulty,
interest, and cognitive demand) that
influences estimation of the passage of
time. Gulliksen (1927) tested levels of
behavior by asking subjects to estimate
the passage of time after each of the
following conditions: at rest, listening
to both rapid and slow metronome beats,

First page of references

Time Estimation   9

References

Axel, R. (1924). Estimation of time.
   Archive of Psychology, 12, 162-176.

Brown, S. W., & West, A. N. (1990).
   Multiple timing and the allocation
   of attention. *Acta Psychologica, 75,*
   103-121.

Carrasco, M.C., Bernal, M.C., & Redolat,
   R. (2001). Time estimation and
   aging: A comparison between young
   and elderly adults. *International
   Journal of Aging & Human
   Development, 52*(2), 91-101. Abstract
   retrieved March 9, 2002, from
   PsycINFO database.

Curton, E. D., & Lordahl, D. S. (1974).
   Effects of attentional focus and
   arousal on time estimation. *Journal
   of Experimental Psychology, 103,*
   861-867.

DeWolfe, R. K. S., & Duncan, C. P.
   (1959). Time estimation as a function of level of behavior of succes-
   sive tasks. *Journal of Experimental
   Psychology, 58,* 153-158.

Gulliksen, H. (1927). The influence of
   occupation upon the perception
   of time. *Journal of Experimental
   Psychology, 10,* 52-59.

12 The CBE Style of Documentation in the Sciences and Mathematics

This section outlines the citation-sequence documentation style recommended by the Council of Biology Editors (CBE) for all scientific disciplines in *Scientific Style and Format: The CBE Manual for Authors, Editors, and Publishers,* 6th ed. (New York: Cambridge UP, 1994).

Basic features of CBE citation-sequence style

KEY POINTS

Two Basic Features of CBE Citation-Sequence Style

1. Give each reference a superscript number in your text, in smaller type than the text of your paper, or include the number on the line within parentheses. Numbers run sequentially throughout your paper.

2. In your list of references at the end of the paper, number the items consecutively in the order in which you mention them in your paper. Do not alphabetize entries. ∎

CBE in-text citations

Include a superscript number to refer readers to your list of references.

```
One summary of studies of the life span of the
    fruit fly¹ has shown that. . . .
```

Refer to more than one entry in the reference list as follows:

```
Two studies of the life span of the fruit fly¹, ²
have shown that....
```

```
Several studies of the life span of the fruit
fly¹⁻⁴ have shown that. . . .
```

See sample reference list in **12d**.

12c CBE sequential list of references

Use the following guidelines when preparing a list of references in CBE style.

 KEY POINTS

What to Do in the CBE List of References

1. Attach a list of references after the last page of your paper headed "References" or "Cited References."

2. Number the items consecutively in the order in which you mention the authors' works in your paper. Invert authors' names and use initials of first names, with no periods separating initials.

3. Begin each entry with the note number followed by a period and a space. Do not indent the first line of each entry; indent subsequent lines to align beneath the first letter of the previous entry.

4. Do not underline or use quotation marks for the titles of articles, books, or journals and other periodicals.

5. Abbreviate titles of journals and organizations.

6. Use a period between major divisions of each entry.

7. Use a semicolon and a space between the name of the publisher and the publication date of a book. Use a semicolon with no space between the date and the volume number of a journal.

8. For books, give the total number of pages, followed by a space and "p." For journal articles, give inclusive page spans, with only as many digits in the second number as are *not* included in the first: 135–6; 287–93; 500–1.

Book with one author

title not underlined,
only first word capitalized

2. Finch CE. Longevity, senescence and

initials with no periods between

abbreviated
publishing terms

the genome. Chicago: Univ Chicago

semicolon   number of pages in book

Pr; 1990. 922 p.

Book with more than one author

8. Ferrini AF, Ferrini RL. Health in the later
   years. 2nd ed. Dubuque (IA): Brown &
   Benchmark; 1993. 470 p.

Article in a scholarly journal

1. Kowald A, Kirkwood TB. Explaining fruit fly
   longevity. Science 1993;260:1664-5.

In a journal paginated by issue, include the issue number in
parentheses after the volume number.

Newspaper or magazine article

6. Altman LK. Study prompts call to halt a
   routine eye operation. NY Times 1995 Feb
   22;Sect C:10.

If no author is named, begin with "[Anonymous]." For an
editorial, insert "[editorial]" after the title.

Electronic journal article Include the type of medium in
brackets after the journal title. Include an availability statement if necessary and the access date.

7. Halbert M. The challenge of multimedia
   networking. Public Access Comput Syst Rev
   [serial online] 1993;4(1):18-23. Available
   from: FTP: lib.ncsu.edu. Accessed 1995
   Feb 28.
9. Van der Heide JC, Paolicelli PB, Boldrini A,
   Cioni G. Kinematic and qualitative analysis
   of lower-extremity movements in preterm
   infants with brain lesions. Phys Ther J
   [serial online] June 1999;79(6). Available
   from: URL: http://www.apta.org/pt_journal/
   June99. Accessed 1999 July 6.

12d CBE paper format: sample list of references

The following list of references for a paper on "Research Findings and Disputes about Fruit Fly Longevity" uses the CBE sequential numbering system. Note the use of abbreviations and punctuation.

```
                    Fruit fly longevity 17
               References
1. Kowald A, Kirkwood TB. Explaining fruit
   fly longevity. Science 1993;260:1664-5.
2. Finch CE. Longevity, senescence and
   the genome. Chicago: Univ Chicago Pr:
   1990. 922 p.
3. Carey JR, Liedo P, Orozco D, Vaupel
   JW. Slowing of mortality rates at
   older ages in large medfly cohorts.
   Science 1992;258:457.
4. Skrecky D. Fly longevity database. CR
   Soc Mailing List [online posting] 1997
   June 22. Available from: URL:
   http://home.clara.net/crooksit/
   msg01958.html. Accessed 1999 Jan 12.
5. Muller H-G, Wang J-L, Capra WB, Liedo
   P, Carey JR. Early mortality surge in
   protein-deprived females causes rever-
   sal of sex differential of life
   expectancy in Mediterranean fruit flies.
   Proc of the Nat Acad of Sci of the US
   [online] 1997 Mar 18;94:2762. Available
   from Infotrac Searchbank: Expanded
   Academic ASAP: URL: http://web3
   .searchbank.com. Accessed 1999 July 7.
```

13 *The Chicago Manual of Style:* System of Endnotes or Footnotes

In addition to an author-year parenthetical system of references similar to the APA system, *The Chicago Manual of Style,* 14th ed. (Chicago: U of Chicago P, 1993) also recommends documenting sources in footnotes or, preferably, endnotes. This system is used widely in the humanities, especially in history, art history, literature, and the arts. For a *Chicago* style paper, include an unnumbered title page, and number the first page of your paper "2."

Basic features of the *Chicago* endnote style

 KEY POINTS

Two Basic Features of the *Chicago* Endnote Style

1. Place a superscript numeral at the end of the quotation or the sentence in which you mention source material; place the number after all punctuation marks except a dash.
2. List all endnotes, double-spaced, on a separate numbered page at the end of the paper, and number the notes sequentially, as they appear in your paper. ∎

13b *Chicago:* in-text citations

Use the following format. Number your notes sequentially.

George Eliot thought that <u>Eliot</u> was a "good, mouth-filling, easy to pronounce word."[5]

See **13c** for the endnote to accompany this citation.

13c *Chicago* endnotes

KEY POINTS

What to Do in the *Chicago* Endnotes

1. In the list of endnotes, place each number on the line (not as a superscript), followed by a period and one space.

2. Indent the first line of each entry three or five spaces.

3. Use the author's full name, not inverted, followed by a comma and the title of the work. Underline book titles (or use an italic font) and use quotation marks around article titles.

4. Capitalize all words in the titles of books and articles except *a, an, the,* coordinating conjunctions, *to* in an infinitive, and prepositions. Capitalize any word that begins or ends the title or subtitle.

5. Follow a book title with publishing information in parentheses followed by a comma and the page number(s), with no "p." or "pp." Follow an article title with the journal or newspaper name and pertinent publication information (volume, issue, date, page numbers). Do not abbreviate months.

6. Separate major parts of the citation with commas, not periods.

First note for a source

        author's name   comma title underlined, all important
   ┌── in normal order──┐\ ┌── words capitalized ──
   5. Margaret Crompton, <u>George Eliot: The</u>
                             comma page number
┐
<u>Woman</u> (London: Cox and Wyman, 1960), 123.

Second reference to the same source, immediately following the first Use "Ibid." (Latin *ibidem,* meaning " in the same place") only to refer to exactly the same author and work as in the previous reference. All the details except the page number should correspond to the previous citation.

   6. Ibid., 127.

Subsequent reference to the same source

    14. Crompton, 124.

Book with one author

    9. Judith Thurman, <u>Isak Dinesen: The Life of a Storyteller</u> (New York: St. Martin's Press, 1982), 80.

Book with two or more authors

    7. George Lakoff and Mark Johnson, <u>Metaphors We Live By</u> (Chicago: University of Chicago Press, 1980), 22.

For a book with more than three authors, use the name of only the first author followed by "et al." (for "and others").

Author of book not named

    5. <u>The Chicago Manual of Style,</u> 14th ed. (Chicago: University of Chicago Press, 1993), 369.

Article in an edited volume

    14. Terrence Des Pres, "Poetry and Politics," in <u>The Writer in Our World,</u> ed. Reginald Gibbons (Boston: Atlantic Monthly Press, 1986), 25.

Article in a scholarly journal

    25. William W. Cook, "Writing in the Spaces Left," <u>College Composition and Communication</u> 44 (1993): 9-25.

When each issue of a journal is paged separately, include the issue number after the volume number: "83, no. 5 (1989)."

Article in a magazine or newspaper Include the month for monthly magazines and the date for weekly magazines and newspapers.

> 9. Philip Elmer-DeWitt, "Battle for the Soul of the Internet," <u>Time,</u> 25 July 1994, 50-56.

Film, filmstrip, slides, or videocassette

> 13. <u>Citizen Kane</u>, prod., written, and dir. Orson Welles, 119 min., RKO, 1941, film.

Online source After any available print information, give the date of online posting, if any; the name of the database, if any; the URL and other retrieval information; and the date you access the material.

> 9. Geoffrey Bent, "Vermeer's Hapless Peer," <u>North American Review</u> 282 (1997), Infotrac Searchbank: Expanded Academic ASAP <http://web2.searchbank.com> (13 January 1999).

13d *Chicago* **paper format: sample endnotes and bibliography page**

Check whether your instructor wants you to include a list of works cited or a bibliography of works consulted in addition to notes. The bibliography begins on a new, numbered page after the endnotes. List entries alphabetically, by authors' last names. Include full names, inverted, not just initials. Indent all lines three or five spaces except the first line of each entry. Double-space throughout. Separate the major parts of each entry with a period and one space. Excerpts of the endnotes and bibliography from a student's paper on the seventeenth-century Dutch painter Pieter de Hooch follow.

Quinones   15
Notes

1. Peter Sutton, <u>Pieter de Hooch:</u>
<u>Complete Edition, with a Catalogue</u>
<u>Raisonné</u> (Ithaca NY: Cornell University
Press, 1980), 44.

    2. Wayne E. Franits, "The Depiction
of Servants in Some Paintings by Pieter
de Hooch," <u>Zeitschrift für</u>
<u>Kunstgeschichte</u> 52 (1989): 560.

Quinones   16
Bibliography

Botton, Alain de. "Domestic Bliss: Pieter
    de Hooch Exhibition." <u>New Statesman</u>,
    9 October 1998: 34-5.

Franits, Wayne E. "The Depiction of
    Servants in Some Paintings by Pieter
    de Hooch." <u>Zeitschrift für</u>
    <u>Kunstgeschichte</u> 52 (1989): 559-66.

Glueck, Grace. "A Loving Home Life, Right
    Down to the Nits." <u>New York Times</u>, 8
    January 1999, E40.

Sutton, Peter. <u>Pieter de Hooch: Complete</u>
    <u>Edition, with a Catalogue Raisonné</u>.
    Ithaca NY: Cornell University Press,
    1980.

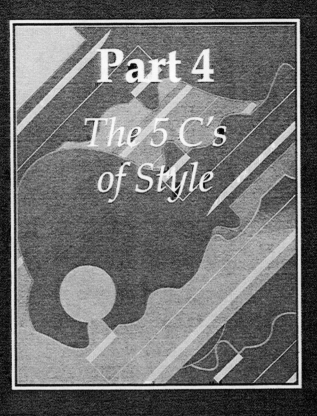

Part 4
The 5 C's of Style

Readers sometimes suffer from what has been called the MEGO reaction to a piece of writing—"My Eyes Glaze Over"—even when ideas are well organized. This reaction happens when readers are bored by wordiness, flatness, inappropriate word choice, clichés, and sentences constructed without interesting variations. Follow the five C's of style to prevent that glazing over.

14 The First C: Cut

Most writing can be improved and even cut to half its original length if you focus on stating your essential ideas and expressing them succinctly. Examine your writing for any unnecessary material, whether ideas, sentences, phrases, or individual words.

14a Cut wordiness.

Say something only once and in the best possible place.

▶ The Lilly Library ~~contains many rare books. The~~
s
~~books in the library are~~ carefully preserved, ~~The~~
many rare books and manuscripts
~~library also houses a manuscript collection.~~

director of
▶ Stephen Spielberg, ~~who has directed~~ the movie ~~that has been~~ described as the best war movie ever made, ~~is someone who~~ knows many politicians.

T
▶ ~~What~~ they ~~do is~~ shop.

▶ California residents have voted to abolish bilingual

education, ~~The main reason for their voting to~~
because
~~abolish bilingual education was that~~ many children

were being placed indiscriminately into programs

and kept there too long.

In addition, trim words that simply repeat an idea expressed in another word in the same phrase: *basic* essentials, *true* facts, circle *around*. Edit redundant pairs: *various and sundry, each and every.*

▶ The task took ~~diligence and~~ perseverance.
has
▶ His surgeon ~~is a doctor~~ with a great deal of clinical experience.

14b Cut formulaic phrases.

Replace wordy phrases with shorter or more direct expressions.

FORMULAIC	NOT FORMULAIC
at the present time	now
at this point in time	
in this day and age	
in today's society	

because of the fact that	because
due to the fact that	
are of the opinion that	believe
have the ability to	can
in spite of the fact that	although, despite
prior to	before
concerning the matter of	about

14c Cut references to your intentions.

Generally, your readers want to read about your topic and are not interested in references to your thinking process. Eliminate references to the organization of your text and your own planning, such as *In this essay, I intend to prove that . . .*; or *In the next few paragraphs, I hope to show that . . .*; *In conclusion, I have demonstrated. . . .*

---

15 The Second C: Check for Action ("Who's Doing What?")

Write vigorous sentences with vivid, expressive verbs rather than bland forms of the verb *be (be, am, is, are, was, were, being, been)* or verbs in the passive voice (**22g**). Use the subject and verb to tell your reader who (or what) is doing what.

15a Ask "Who's doing what?" about subject and verb.

Let the subject of your sentence perform the action.

WORDY   **The mayor's approval of the new law was due to the voters' suspicion of the concealment of campaign funds by his deputy.**

Ask "Who's doing what?"

SUBJECT	VERB
the mayor	approved
the voters	suspected
his deputy	had concealed

REVISED   **The mayor approved the new law because the voters suspected that his deputy had concealed campaign funds.**

15b Use caution in beginning a sentence with *there* or *it*.

Rewriting a sentence that begins with *there* often makes the sentence leaner and more direct. Revise by using a verb that shows action and a subject that "does" the action.

WORDY   **There was a discussion of the health care system by the politicians.**

Who's doing what here?

REVISED **The politicians discussed the health care system.**

WORDY   **It is clear that Baker admires Updike.**

REVISED **Clearly, Baker admires Updike.**

 In some languages, an *it* subject can be omitted. It must be included in English. See also **19c.**

    it
► She went to the park because ‸was a warm day. ■

15c Avoid unnecessary passive voice constructions.

The passive voice tells what is done to the grammatical subject of the sentence ("The turkey *was cooked* too long"). Extensive use of the passive voice can make your style dull and wordy.

PASSIVE **The problem will be discussed thoroughly by the committee.**

REVISED **The committee will discuss the problem thoroughly.**

The passive voice occurs frequently in scientific writing where readers are primarily interested in data, procedures, and results, not in who developed or produced them. In a scientific report, you are likely to read, for example, *The rats were fed*, not *The researchers fed the rats*. See **22g** for more on the passive voice.

 Note that only a transitive verb can be used in the passive voice.

► An accident ~~was~~ happened at the corner. ■

16 The Third C: Connect

Coherent paragraphs are ones in which information that has been mentioned before is connected to new information in a smooth flow, not a series of grasshopperlike jumps.

16a Apply the principle of consistent subjects.

Readers need to have a way to connect the ideas beginning a sentence with what has gone before. From one sentence to the next, avoid jarring shifts of subjects.

JARRING SHIFT
Memoirs **are becoming increasingly popular.** *Readers* **all over the continent are finding them appealing.**

REVISED
Memoirs **are becoming increasingly popular.** *They* **appeal to readers all over the continent.**

16b Connect with transitional words and expressions.

The following words and expressions provide logical connections between sentences and paragraphs.

TRANSITIONAL WORDS AND EXPRESSIONS

Adding an idea: also, in addition, further, furthermore, moreover

Contrasting: however, nevertheless, nonetheless, on the other hand, in contrast, still, on the contrary, rather, conversely

Providing an alternative: instead, alternatively, otherwise

Showing similarity: similarly, likewise

Showing order of time or order of ideas: first, second, third (and so on), then, next, later, subsequently, meanwhile, previously, finally

Showing result: as a result, consequently, therefore, thus, hence, accordingly, for this reason

Affirming: of course, in fact, certainly, obviously, to be sure, undoubtedly, indeed

Giving examples: for example, for instance

Explaining: in other words, that is

Adding an aside: incidentally, by the way, besides

Summarizing: in short, generally, overall, all in all, in conclusion, above all

For punctuation with transitional words and expressions, see **26a**.

16c Vary the way you connect and combine your ideas.

To express an idea, you have alternatives. Vary the methods you use to show the connections between ideas, as in the following examples:

► Brillo pads work well. I don't give them as gifts.

► Brillo pads work well, but I don't give them as gifts.

► Although Brillo pads work well, I don't give them as gifts.

► Brillo pads work well; however, I don't give them as gifts.

16d Connect paragraphs.

A new paragraph signals a shift to a new topic, but not necessarily to one that is completely different. Use the following strategies to connect your ideas:

1. Read your draft aloud. As you finish a paragraph, note what point you made in the paragraph. Then, at the end, check your flow and logic.

2. Refer to the main idea of the previous paragraph as you begin the next. After a paragraph on retirement, the next paragraph might begin like this: *Retirement is not the only reason for saving. Saving also provides a nest egg for the unexpected and the pleasurable.*

3. Use transitions such as *also, too, in addition, however, therefore,* and *as a result* to signal the logical connection between paragraphs (**16b**).

17 The Fourth C: Commit

Readers of academic prose in English usually expect writers to analyze and question their sources, to commit to an informed and interesting point of view (not necessarily to the dominant view), and to provide convincing reasons why that view is valid. For writers, commitment means researching and considering an issue, assuming a critical stance, taking a position, and persuasively supporting that position.

17a Commit to critical thinking.

Critical thinking does not mean criticizing negatively. It means examining and analyzing information with an open mind. When you think critically, your writing takes on your own voice, your own stance.

Do the following to develop your critical thinking skills: Observe and remember details; write frequent journal entries on your observations, reading, and ideas; ask questions; look for assumptions and bias in the words of others; try to understand the reasoning behind viewpoints you disagree with; analyze and evaluate how arguments are presented.

17b Commit to a point of view.

Use language that shows commitment to the point of view you develop through your critical thinking. When you are trying to persuade your readers to accept your point of view, avoid the language of ambivalence and indecisiveness evident in words and phrases like *maybe, perhaps, might, it could be, it could happen, it might seem,* and *it would appear.* Aim for language that reflects accountability and commitment: *as a result, consequently, of course, believe, need, demand, think, should, must.* Use language of commitment, however, only after you have thoroughly researched your topic and found the evidence convincing.

18 The Fifth C: Choose Vivid, Appropriate, and Inclusive Words

Word choice, or *diction,* contributes a great deal to the effect your writing has on a reader. Do not give your reader puzzles to solve.

18a Choose vivid and specific words.

Choosing vivid words means avoiding clichés. Avoid sayings that have been heard and read too often, like *hit the nail on the head, crystal clear, better late than never,* and *easier said than done.* Use words that are vivid, descriptive, and specific. Provide details to create visual images for your readers. General words such as *area, aspect, certain* ("a certain expression," for example), *circumstance, factor, kind, manner, nature, situation, nice,* and *thing* are vague and do not give a reader much information.

VAGUE **The girl in Kincaid's story "Girl" did many things often regarded as women's jobs.**

[*Things* is a vague word.]

SPECIFIC **The girl in the story did many household chores often regarded as women's work: She washed the clothes, cooked, swept, set the table, and cleared away dishes.**

18b Avoid slang, regionalisms, and jargon.

Slang When you write college essays, your tone and diction should consistently be formal rather than colloquial. Avoid slang and colloquial expressions, such as *folks, guy, OK, okay, pretty good, hassle, kind of interesting/nice, too big of a deal, a lot of, lots of, a ways away.* Do not enclose a slang expression in quotation marks to signal to your readers that you know it is inappropriate. Instead, revise.

▶ The working conditions were "gross." *disgusting*

▶ I did real super in my last job. *well*

▶ The jury returned the verdict that the guy was not guilty. *defendant*

Regional language Use regional and ethnic dialects in writing only when you are quoting someone directly: *"Your car needs fixed," he advised.* Otherwise, use standard forms.

▶ I bought me a camcorder. *myself*

▶ She used to could run two miles, but now she's out of shape. *be able to*

Jargon Most areas of specialized work and study have their own technical words, which people outside those fields perceive as jargon. A sportswriter writing about baseball will, for instance, refer to *twinight doubleheaders, ERAs,* and *brushbacks.* A linguist writing about language will use terms like *phonemics, kinesics,* and *suprasegmentals.* If you know that your audience is familiar with the technical vocabulary of the field, specialized language is acceptable. Try to avoid jargon when writing for a more general audience; if you must use technical terms, provide definitions that will make sense to your audience.

18c Avoid biased and exclusionary language.

Do not use divisive terms that reinforce stereotypes or belittle other people. Do not emphasize differences by separating society into *we* to refer to people like you and *they* or *these people* to refer to people different from you. Use *we* only to be truly inclusive of yourself and all your readers. Be aware, too, of terms that are likely to offend. You don't have to be excessive in your zeal to be PC ("politically correct"), using *underachieve* for *fail,* or *vertically challenged* for *short,* but do your best to avoid alienating readers.

Gender   The writer of the following sentence edited to avoid gender bias in the perception of women's roles and achievements.

> ▶ ~~Mrs. John~~ Andrea Harrison, ~~married to a real-estate tycoon and herself the bubbly, blonde~~ chief executive of a successful computer company, has expanded the business overseas.

Choice of words can reveal gender bias, too.

AVOID	USE
actress	actor
authoress	author
chairman	chairperson
female astronaut	astronaut
forefathers	ancestors
foreman	supervisor
mailman	mail carrier
male nurse	nurse

man, mankind (meaning any human being)	person, people, our species, human beings, humanity
manmade	synthetic
policeman, policewoman	police officer
salesman	sales representative, salesclerk
veterans and their wives	veterans and their spouses

With the use of pronouns, too, avoid the stereotyping that occurs by assigning gender roles to professions, such as *he* for a doctor or lawyer, and *she* for a nurse or a secretary.

or she
▶ Before a surgeon can operate, he must know every detail of the patient's history.

However, often it is better to avoid the *he* or *she* issue by recasting the sentence or using a plural noun or pronoun.

▶ Before operating, a surgeon must know every detail of the patient's history.

▶ Before surgeons can operate, they must know every detail of the patient's history.

See **24c** for more on pronouns and gender.

Race and place Name a person's race only when it is relevant.

▶ Attending the meeting were three doctors and an ~~Asian~~ computer programmer.

Use the names people prefer for their racial or ethnic affiliation. Consider, for example, that *black* and *African American* are preferred terms; *Native American* is preferred to *American Indian; Asian* is preferred to *Oriental*. Be careful, too, with the way you refer to countries and continents; the Americas include both North and South America. Avoid stereotyping people according to where they come from. Some British people may be stiff and formal, but not all are. Not all Germans eat sausage and drink beer; not all North Americans carry cameras and wear plaid shorts.

Age   Avoid derogatory, condescending, or disrespectful terms associated with age. Refer to a person's age or condition neutrally, if at all: not *well-preserved little old lady* but *woman in her eighties* or just *woman.*

Politics   Words referring to politics are full of connotations. The word *liberal,* for instance, has been used with positive and negative connotations in various election campaigns. Take care with words like *radical, left-wing, right-wing,* and *moderate.* Are you identifying with one group and implicitly criticizing other groups?

Religion   An old edition of an encyclopedia referred to "devout Catholics" and "fanatical Muslims." The new edition refers to both Catholics and Muslims as "devout," thus eliminating biased language. Examine your use of words that sound derogatory or exclusionary, such as *cult* or *fundamentalist,* and terms—such as *these people*—that emphasize difference, or even the word *we* when it implies that all your readers share (or should share) your beliefs.

Health and abilities   Avoid terms like *confined to a wheelchair* and *victim* (of a disease), so as not to focus on difference and disability. Instead, write *someone who uses a wheelchair* and *person with* (a disease). Do not draw unnecessary attention to a disability or an illness.

Sexual orientation   Refer to a person's sexual orientation only if the information is necessary to your content. To say that someone was "defended by a homosexual lawyer" is gratuitous when describing a case of stock market fraud, but more relevant in a case of discrimination against homosexuals. Since you will not necessarily know your readers' sexual orientation, do not assume it is the same as your own, and beware of using terms and making comments that might offend.

The word normal   One word to be especially careful about using is *normal*—when referring to your own health, ability, or sexual orientation. Some readers could justifiably find that offensive.

Part 5
Common Sentence Problems

105

Part 5 Common Sentence Problems

19 Sentence Fragments

A fragment is an incomplete sentence that is incorrectly punctuated as if it were a complete sentence. A complete sentence must have an independent clause with a subject and verb. Usually you can fix a fragment by connecting it to a closely related independent clause in your text or by completing the fragment so it can stand alone.

19a Phrase fragments

A phrase is a group of words without a subject or a verb or both. If a phrase is punctuated as a sentence, it is a phrase fragment. Correct phrase fragments in any of the following ways:

1. Attach the phrase to a nearby independent clause to form a complete sentence.

   ▶ He wanted to make a point, ~~To~~ *to* prove to everyone that he was capable.

   ▶ The researcher's principle was carefully *of confidentiality* upheld. ~~The principle of confidentiality.~~

   ▶ The house was still standing, ~~On~~ *o*n the corner, next to the elm tree.

2. Change the phrase to an independent clause.

   ▶ Nature held many attractions for Thoreau. Especially, *he valued* the solitude.

3. Rewrite the whole passage.

   ▶ Ralph ~~talked for hours. Elated~~ *was so elated* by the company's success, *that he talked for hours.*

19b Dependent clause fragments

A dependent clause beginning with a subordinating word such as *because, if, unless, when, as soon as, whenever, while, although, that, which,* or *who* (or with a question word such as *how, what,* or *why*) cannot stand alone and be punctuated as an independent clause. Choose whichever of the following two methods of repair works better.

1. Connect the dependent clause to a nearby independent clause.

   ▶ The town takes on a festive air/ ᵂWhen the circus arrives.

2. Delete the subordinating conjunction at the beginning of the dependent clause. The dependent clause then becomes an independent clause, which can stand alone.

   ▶ The author describes her family life with her

   parents and seven siblings. ~~How~~ ꜱshe grew up

   following her parents' values.

NOTE: A subordinating conjunction at the beginning of a sentence does not always signal a fragment. A correctly punctuated sentence may begin with a subordinating conjunction introducing a dependent clause, but the sentence will also contain an independent clause.

   ┌──────────── dependent clause ────────────┐ ┌───────────
   ▶ Because Lars liked to make people laugh, he became
   ─ independent clause ─┐
   a stand-up comic.

19c Missing verb, verb part, or subject

Every sentence must contain a complete verb (one that shows tense) in an independent clause. If a word group punctuated as a sentence lacks a verb or has an incomplete verb, it is a fragment. Supply all necessary forms or recast the sentence.

▶ The writing is hard to understand. Too many
        have
commas␣been left out.
        ^

           are
▶ Some people␣eager to live in a big city.
           ^

    A word group appearing without a subject is also a fragment. Correct as follows:

1. Include an appropriate subject. Never omit an *it* or *there* filler subject. See **15b** and **36a**.

   It is
   ▶ ~~Is~~ advisable to exercise every day.
     ^

2. Turn the fragment into a phrase and attach it to the independent clause.

               looking
   ▶ The commuters waited, ~~Looked~~ hopefully
      down the track.

3. One subject cannot be the subject of two verbs across two sentences. Correct a fragment beginning with *And* or *But* by removing the period and capital letter; the second verb then is attached to the subject in the independent clause, creating a compound predicate.

                            and
   ▶ After an hour, the dancers changed partners,
      ~~And~~ adapted to a different type of music.

19d Intentional fragments

Fragments are used frequently in advertisements to keep the text short. In academic writing, writers sometimes use a fragment intentionally for emphasis after a question, as an exclamation, or at a point of transition.

▶ Is the president always truthful? Not entirely.

In college essays, use intentional fragments sparingly, if at all.

20 Run-ons and Comma Splices

20a Identifying run-on (or *fused*) sentences and comma splices

If two independent clauses run together without any punctuation between them, the error is called a *run-on sentence* or *fused sentence*. If only a comma appears between them with no coordinating conjunction, such as *and* or *but*, the error is called a *comma splice*. A comma splice error also occurs when a comma and a transitional expression such as *however* and *in fact* join two independent clauses (**16b**).

20b Five methods for correcting run-on sentences and comma splices

Select the method that works best for the sentence you are editing.

Method 1 Separate the two independent clauses into two sentences, each with its own end mark.

▶ Beavers cut down trees with their teeth, ~~they~~ use the
  They
  trees for food and shelter.

Method 2 Separate the two independent clauses with a semicolon if the clauses are connected by a transitional word or expression such as *however* or *therefore*.

▶ Willow trees are beautiful; however, their branches are weak.

Method 3 Separate the two independent clauses with a comma and a coordinating conjunction (*and, but, or, nor, so, for, yet*).

▶ Woodpeckers look for insects in trees, but they do not intentionally destroy live trees.

Method 4 Make one clause dependent on the other by adding a subordinating conjunction.

> Whenever the
> ▶ ~~The~~ beavers dammed up the river, the rise in the
> ^
> water level destroyed the trees.

Method 5 Make one clause into a phrase containing an
-ing form and attach it to the remaining independent clause.

> jumping
> ▶ Salmon swim upstream, ~~they jump~~ over huge dams
> to reach their destination.

21 Sentence Snarls

Avoid or edit sentences with structural inconsistencies that
make readers pause to untangle the meaning.

21a Tangles: mixed constructions, faulty comparisons, and convoluted syntax

Mixed constructions A mixed construction is a sentence with parts incompatible in grammar and meaning.
The sentence begins one way and then veers off in an unexpected direction. Check that the subject and verb in your
sentence are clear and work together. Do not use a pronoun
to restate the subject (**36a** ESL).

> The
> ▶ ~~In the~~ excerpt by Heilbrun and the story by Gould
> are similar.

> S
> ▶ ~~By~~ sleeping late can create tension with parents.

> ▶ Dinah Macy ~~she~~ got Lyme disease when she was ten.

When you start a sentence with an adverb clause (beginning
with a word like *when, if, because,* and *since*), make sure you
follow that clause with an independent clause. An adverb
clause cannot serve as the subject of a verb.

> Swimming
> ▶ ~~Because she swims~~ every day does not guarantee she
> is healthy.

Trading
▶ ~~When~~ a player ~~is traded~~ often causes family problems.

 For sentences beginning with *although*, see **36d** ESL. ■

Faulty comparisons When you make comparisons, your reader needs to know clearly what you are comparing. See also **24a** for faulty comparisons with personal pronouns.

FAULTY COMPARISON	**Like Wallace Stevens, her job strikes readers as unexpected for a poet.** [It is not her job that is like the poet Wallace Stevens; her job is like his job.]
REVISED	**Like Wallace Stevens, she holds a job that strikes readers as unexpected for a poet.**

Convoluted syntax Revise sentences that ramble on to such an extent that they become tangled. Make sure they have clear subjects, verbs, and connections between clauses.

TANGLED	**The way I feel about getting what you want is that when there is a particular position or item that you want to try to get to do your best and not give up because if you give up you have probably missed your chance of succeeding.**
POSSIBLE REVISION	**To get what you want, keep trying.**

21b Misplaced modifiers

Keep words, phrases, and clauses that provide adjectival or adverbial information next to the sentence element that they modify. That is, avoid *misplaced modifiers*.

Take care with words such as only. Place a word such as *only, even, just, nearly, merely,* or *simply* immediately before the word it modifies. The meaning of a sentence can change significantly as the position of *only* changes, so careful placement is important.

▶ *Only* the journalist began to investigate the incident. [no one else]

▶ The journalist *only* began to investigate the incident. [but didn't finish]

▶ The journalist began to investigate *only* the incident. [nothing else]

Place a phrase or clause close to the word it modifies.

MISPLACED | **They sent a present to their mother wrapped in silver paper.** [This sentence gives the impression that the mother was wrapped in silver paper.]

POSSIBLE REVISIONS | **They sent their mother a present wrapped in silver paper.**

They sent a present wrapped in silver paper to their mother.

Consider the case for splitting an infinitive. You split an infinitive when you place a word or phrase between *to* and the verb. *The New Oxford Dictionary of English* finds the use of split infinitives "both normal and useful," as in "To boldly go where no man has gone before . . ." (*Star Trek*). However, such splitting may irritate readers, especially when a clumsy sentence is the result.

┌──────── split infinitive *(to inform)* ────────
▶ We want to sincerely, honestly, and in confidence
└──────┐
inform you of our plans for expansion.

21c Dangling modifiers

An adjectival modifier that is not grammatically linked to the noun or phrase it is intended to describe is said to *dangle*. An *-ing* or *-ed* modifier beginning a sentence needs to tell about the subject of the sentence.

DANGLING | **Walking into the house, the telephone rang.** [Who was walking? The sentence says it was the telephone.]

REVISED | **Walking into the house, we heard the telephone ring.**

While we were walking into the house, the telephone rang.

21d Shifts

Do not shift abruptly from statements to commands.

▶ Students need to be more aggressive. ~~Ask~~ more
questions and challenge the professors.

> They should ask

Do not shift from indirect to direct quotation, with or without quotation marks.

▶ The client told us that he wanted to sign the lease

and ~~would we~~ prepare the papers.

> asked us to

Do not shift tenses unnecessarily.

▶ Some lawyers advance their careers by honest hard
work. Others ~~represented~~ famous clients.

Do not shift point of view.   Be consistent in using first,
second, or third person pronouns.

▶ We all need a high salary to live in a city because
~~you~~ have to spend so much on rent and

> we

transportation.

21e Logical sequence after the subject

Do not use a subject and predicate (verb and object or complement) that do not make logical sense together.

▶ ~~The decision to build~~ an elaborate extension onto the
train station made all the trains arrive late. [It was not
the decision that delayed the trains, but the building
of the extension.]

> Building

▶ According to the guidelines, ~~people in~~ dilapidated
buildings will be demolished this year. [The
building, not people, will be demolished.]

21f Parallel structures

Balance your sentences by using similar grammatical constructions in each part.

NOT PARALLEL | **The results of reform were that class size decreased, more multicultural courses, and being allowed to choose a pass/fail option.**

PARALLEL | **The results of reform were that class size decreased, more multicultural courses were offered, and students were allowed to choose a pass/fail option.**

PARALLEL | **The results of reform were a decrease in class size, an increase in the number of multicultural courses, and the introduction of a pass/fail option for students.**

Use parallel structures in comparisons with *as* or *than* and in lists.

To drive
▶ ~~Driving~~ to Cuernavaca is as expensive as to take the bus.

Taking
▶ ~~To take~~ the bus is less comfortable than driving.

▶ Writing well demands the following: (1) planning

revising
your time, (2) paying attention to details, (3) ~~the need~~
∧

~~for revision,~~ and (4) proofreading.

21g Definitions and reasons: avoiding *is when* and *the reason is because*

When you write a definition of a term, avoid using *is when* or *is where* (or *was when, was where*).

▶ A tiebreak in tennis *is ~~where there's~~* a final game to decide a set.

In writing about reasons, avoid *the reason is because*. . . .

Grammatically, an adverb clause beginning with *because* cannot follow the verb *be*. Instead, use *the reason is that . . .* or recast the sentence.

FAULTY   *The reason* **Venus Williams lost** *is because* **her opponent was serving so well.**

POSSIBLE REVISIONS   *The reason* **Williams lost** *is that* **her opponent was serving so well.**

Williams lost *because* **her opponent was serving so well.**

Note that standard English requires *the reason (that)* and not *the reason why*.

▶ **The TV commentator explained the reason** ~~why~~ **Williams lost.**

21h Necessary words in compound structures and comparisons

Do not omit necessary words in compound structures. If you omit a verb form from a compound verb, the remaining verb form must fit into each part of the compound; otherwise, you must use the complete verb form.

      tried
▶ **He has always and will always try to preserve his father's good name in the community.** [*Try* fits only with *will*, not with *has*.]

Do not omit necessary words in comparisons.

      as
▶ **The volleyball captain is as competitive or even more competitive than her teammates.** [The comparative structures are *as competitive as* and *more competitive than*. Do not merge them.]

Sometimes you create ambiguity for your readers if you omit the verb in the second part of a comparison.

      did
▶ **He liked baseball more than his son.** [Omitting *did* implies that he liked baseball more than he liked his son.]

22 Verbs

Identify a verb by checking that the base form (that is, the form found as a dictionary entry) fits one or more of these sentences. For example, *vary* will fit; *variety* will not.

They want to ——————. It is going to ————.

They will ——————. It will ————.

Verbs tell readers what people or things do and are. Changes in form and tense can convey subtle distinctions, so edit verbs with care.

22a Verb forms in standard English

All verbs except *be* and modal verbs such as *must* and *can* (**22b**) have five forms. For *regular verbs*, the five forms follow a regular and predictable pattern. Once you know the base form, you can construct all the other forms, using the auxiliaries *be*, *do*, and *have*.

> Base form: the form in a dictionary; used in present tense or after *do* and modal verbs
>
> *-s* form: the third person singular form of the present tense
>
> *-ing* form: also known as the *present participle*; needs auxiliary verbs to form a complete verb phrase; can also appear in a phrase (*Looking* happy, she accepted the award) and as a noun (gerund—*Waiting* is boring)
>
> Past tense form: forms a complete verb; used without auxiliaries
>
> Past participle form: needs auxiliary verbs to form a complete verb phrase (*has chosen, was chosen*); can appear in a phrase (*the chosen few; chosen for her efficiency*)

For *be*, *do*, *have*, and modal verbs, see **22b**.

REGULAR VERBS				
BASE	**-s**	**-Ing PRESENT PARTICIPLE**	**PAST TENSE**	**PAST PARTICIPLE**
paint	paints	painting	painted	painted
smile	smiles	smiling	smiled	smiled

Irregular verbs do not use *-ed* to form the past tense and the past participle. See the following table for forms of irregular verbs, including the verb *be*.

IRREGULAR VERBS

BASE FORM	PAST TENSE	PAST PARTICIPLE
arise	arose	arisen
be	was/were	been
beat	beat	beaten
become	became	become
begin	began	begun
bend	bent	bent
bet	bet	bet (or betted)
bind	bound	bound
bite	bit	bitten
bleed	bled	bled
blow	blew	blown
break	broke	broken
bring	brought	brought
build	built	built
burst	burst	burst
buy	bought	bought
catch	caught	caught
choose	chose	chosen
cling	clung	clung
come	came	come
cost	cost	cost
creep	crept	crept
cut	cut	cut
deal	dealt	dealt
dig	dug	dug
do	did	done
draw	drew	drawn
drink	drank	drunk
drive	drove	driven
eat	ate	eaten
fall	fell	fallen
feed	fed	fed
feel	felt	felt
fight	fought	fought

BASE FORM	PAST TENSE	PAST PARTICIPLE
find	found	found
flee	fled	fled
fly	flew	flown
forbid	forbad(e)	forbidden
forget	forgot	forgotten
forgive	forgave	forgiven
freeze	froze	frozen
get	got	gotten, got
give	gave	given
go	went	gone
grind	ground	ground
grow	grew	grown
hang*	hung	hung
have	had	had
hear	heard	heard
hide	hid	hidden
hit	hit	hit
hold	held	held
hurt	hurt	hurt
keep	kept	kept
know	knew	known
lay	laid	laid (see also 22c)
lead	led	led
leave	left	left
lend	lent	lent
let	let	let
lie	lay	lain (see also 22c)
light	lit, lighted	lit, lighted
lose	lost	lost
make	made	made
mean	meant	meant
meet	met	met
put	put	put
quit	quit	quit
read	read	read
ride	rode	ridden
ring	rang	rung
rise	rose	risen (see also 22c)

Hang in the sense of "put to death" is regular: *hang, hanged, hanged.*

BASE FORM	PAST TENSE	PAST PARTICIPLE
run	ran	run
say	said	said
see	saw	seen
seek	sought	sought
sell	sold	sold
send	sent	sent
set	set	set (see also 22c)
shake	shook	shaken
shine	shone	shone
shoot	shot	shot
shrink	shrank	shrunk
shut	shut	shut
sing	sang	sung
sink	sank	sunk
sit	sat	sat (see also 22c)
sleep	slept	slept
slide	slid	slid
slit	slit	slit
speak	spoke	spoken
spend	spent	spent
spin	spun	spun
spit	spit, spat	spit
split	split	split
spread	spread	spread
spring	sprang	sprung
stand	stood	stood
steal	stole	stolen
stick	stuck	stuck
sting	stung	stung
stink	stank (or stunk)	stunk
strike	struck	struck, stricken
swear	swore	sworn
sweep	swept	swept
swim	swam	swum
swing	swung	swung
take	took	taken
teach	taught	taught
tear	tore	torn
tell	told	told
think	thought	thought

BASE FORM	PAST TENSE	PAST PARTICIPLE
throw	threw	thrown
tread	trod	trodden, trod
understand	understood	understood
upset	upset	upset
wake	woke	waked, woken
wear	wore	worn
weave	wove	woven
weep	wept	wept
win	won	won
wind	wound	wound
wring	wrung	wrung
write	wrote	written

22b Verb forms after auxiliaries

An independent clause needs a *complete verb*. Verb forms such as the *-ing* form and the past participle are not complete, because they do not show tense. They need auxiliary verbs to complete their meaning as a verb of a clause.

AUXILIARY VERBS	MODAL AUXILIARY VERBS	
do: does, do, did	will, would	shall, should
be: be, am, is, are, was, were, being, been	can, could	may, might, must
have: has, have, had		

Auxiliary verbs and modal auxiliary verbs can be used in combination. Whatever the combination, the verb form immediately following the final auxiliary or modal verb is fixed: base form, *-ing*, or past participle.

WHICH FORM SHOULD I USE?

1. After *do, does, did,* and the nine modal verbs—*will, would, can, could, shall, should, may, might,* and *must*—use the base form.

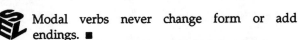 Modal verbs never change form or add endings. ■

▶ He might stay.   ▶ They must eat soon.

▶ Did she leave?   ▶ He could try.

2. After *has, have,* and *had,* use the past participle.

▶ It *has snowed.*

▶ They should *have gone* (not "They should have went").

▶ They *had eaten* when I arrived.

In informal speech, we run sounds together, and the pronunciation may be mistakenly carried over into writing.

▶ She should <s>of</s> ^have^ left that job last year.

The pronunciation of the contraction *should've* is probably responsible for the nonstandard form *should of.* Edit carefully for the appearance of the word *of* in place of *have* in verb phrases.

3. After *be, am, is, are, was, were,* and *been,* use the *-ing* form for active voice verbs.

▶ She *is taking* her driving test.

▶ You *were watching.*

▶ He might have *been driving.*

▶ They could *be jogging.*

Always use a *be* auxiliary before the *-ing* form. The *-ing* form alone can never be a complete verb in a clause.

▶ The crowds ^are^ gathering. ■

4. After *be, am, is, are, was, were, been,* and *being,* use the past participle for passive voice (see **22g**).

▶ They *were taken* to a tropical island for their anniversary.

▶ The faucet should *be fixed.*

▶ The cake might have *been eaten.*

▶ The house is *being decorated.*

Be requires a modal before it to form a complete verb (*could be jogging; will be closed*). *Been* requires *have, has,* or *had* (*have been driving; has been eaten*). *Being* must be preceded by *am, is, are, was,* or *were* to form a complete verb and must be followed by a past participle: *He was being followed.* ■

22c Verbs commonly confused

You may need to give special attention to the forms of certain verbs that are similar but have different meanings. Some verbs can or should be followed by a direct object; these are called *transitive verbs*. Some verbs, however, can never be followed by a direct object; these are called *intransitive verbs*.

1. *rise:* to get up; ascend (intransitive)

   raise: to lift, to cause to rise (transitive)

BASE	–s	–ing	PAST TENSE	PAST PARTICIPLE
rise	rises	rising	rose	risen
raise	raises	raising	raised	raised

2. *sit:* to be seated (intransitive)

   set: to put or place (transitive)

sit	sits	sitting	sat	sat
set	sets	setting	set	set

3. *lie:* to recline (intransitive)

   lay: to put or place (transitive)

lie	lies	lying	lay	lain
lay	lays	laying	laid	laid

   ▶ The sun *rose* at 5:55 A.M. today.

   ▶ She *raised* the blind and peeked out.

   ▶ He *sat* on the wooden chair.

   ▶ She *set* the vase in the middle of the shelf.

       lay
   ▶ I ~~laid~~ down for half an hour.

lying
► I was ~~laying~~ down when you called.

Lay
► ~~Lie~~ the map on the floor.

In addition, note the verb *lie* ("to say something untrue"), which is intransitive:

BASE	-s	-ing	PAST TENSE	PAST PARTICIPLE
lie	lies	lying	lied	lied

► He *lied* when he said he had won three trophies.

22d Verb tenses

Tenses and time are closely related. Verbs change form to indicate present or past time. Auxiliary verbs (*be*, *do*, and *have*) are used with the main verb to convey completed actions (perfect forms), actions in progress (progressive forms), and actions that are completed by some specified time or event and that emphasize the length of time in progress (perfect progressive forms).

Simple present Use the simple present tense for the following purposes:

1. To make a generalization

   ► We *turn* the clocks ahead every April.

2. To indicate an activity that happens habitually or repeatedly

   ► He *works* for Sony.

   ► They *take* vacations in Puerto Rico.

3. To express future time in dependent clauses (clauses beginning with subordinating words such as *if, when, before, after, until, as soon as*) when *will* is used in the independent clause

   ► When they *arrive*, the meeting will begin.

4. To discuss literature and the arts (called the *literary present*) even though the work was written in the past or the author is no longer alive

▶ In *Zami,* Audre Lorde *describes* how a librarian *introduces* her to the joys of reading.

However, when you write a narrative of your own, use past tenses to tell about past actions.

▶ Then the candidate ~~walks~~ *walked* up to the crowd and ~~kisses~~ *kissed* all the babies.

5. 🎐 To refer to ideas of mental activity, appearance, and inclusion

Do not use progressive forms with intransitive verbs such as *smell, prefer, understand, own, seem,* and *contain.*

▶ They ~~are possessing~~ *possess* different behavior patterns. ■

Present progressive   Use the present progressive to indicate an action in progress at the moment of speaking or writing.

▶ He is *playing* pool with his nephew.

Present perfect and present perfect progressive   Use the present perfect (*has* or *have* followed by a past participle) in the following instances:

1. To indicate that an action occurring at some unstated time in the past is related to present time

   ▶ They *have worked* in New Mexico, so they know its laws.

2. To indicate that an action beginning in the past continues to the present

   ▶ They *have worked* in New Mexico for three years.

However, if you state the exact time when something occurred, use the simple past tense, not the present perfect.

▶ They ~~have~~ worked in Arizona four years ago.

3. To report research results in APA style

▶ Feynmann *has shown* that science can be fun.

Use the present perfect progressive when you indicate the length of time an action is in progress up to the present time.

▶ They *have been dancing* for three hours. [This sentence implies that they are still dancing.]

Simple past   Use the simple past tense when you specify exactly when an event occurred or when you illustrate a general principle with a specific incident in the past.

▶ She *married* him last month.

▶ Some bilingual schools offer intensive instruction in English. My sister *went* to a bilingual school where she *studied* English for two hours every day.

When the sequence of past events is indicated with words like *before* or *after*, use the simple past for both events.

▶ She *knew* how to write her name before she *went* to school.

Use past tenses in an indirect quotation introduced by a past tense verb.

▶ Our lawyer *told* us that the meetings *were* over.

Past progressive   Use the past progressive for an activity in progress over time or at a specified point in the past.

▶ He *was lifting* weights when I called.

Past perfect and past perfect progressive   Use the past perfect or past perfect progressive when one past event was completed before another past event.

▶ He *had cooked* the whole meal by the time Sam arrived. [Two events occurred: he cooked the meal; then Sam arrived.]

▶ He *had been cooking* for three hours when his sister finally offered to help. [An event in progress—cooking—was interrupted in the past.]

▶ The professor announced that she *had revised* the syllabus.

22e Past tense and past participle forms

With regular verbs, both the past tense form and the past participle form end in *-ed*. This ending can cause writers trouble, since in speech the ending is often dropped—particularly when it blends into the next sound.

▶ They wash^ed two baskets of laundry last night.

Standard English requires the *-ed* ending in the following instances.

1. To form the past tense of a regular verb

   ▶ He ask^ed to leave early.

2. To form the past participle of a regular verb for use with the auxiliary *has, have,* or *had* in the active voice or with forms of *be (am, is, are, was, were, be, being, been)* in the passive voice (see 22g)

   ▶ She has work^ed there for a long time.   [Active]

   ▶ The work will be finish^ed tomorrow.   [Passive]

3. To form a past participle for use as an adjective

   ▶ Put in some chop^ped meat. ▶ The frighten^ed boy ran away.

   ▶ I was surprise^d to read how many awards he had won.

NOTE: The following *-ed* forms are used after forms of *be*: *concerned, confused, depressed, divorced, embarrassed, married, prejudiced, satisfied, scared, supposed (to), surprised, used (to), worried.* See also 35e.

▶ He use^d to play third base; now he pitches.

▶ They were suppose^d to call their parents when they arrived.

Do not confuse the past tense and past participle forms of irregular verbs. A past tense form occurs alone as a complete verb, and a past participle form must be used with a *have* or *be* auxiliary.

      drank
▶ He ~~drunk~~ too much last night.

      did
▶ She ~~done~~ her best.

        gone
▶ You could have ~~went~~ alone.

        rung
▶ The bell was ~~rang~~ five times.

22f Verbs in conditional sentences, wishes, requests, demands, and recommendations

Conditions   When *if* or *unless* is used to introduce a dependent clause, the sentence expresses a condition. Four types of conditional sentences are used in English; two refer to actual or possible situations, and two refer to speculative or hypothetical situations. The following box gives examples of the four types of conditional sentences.

KEY POINTS

Verb Tenses in Conditional Sentences

MEANING EXPRESSED	*IF* CLAUSE	INDEPENDENT CLAUSE
1. Fact	Simple present	Simple present

▶ If people *earn* more, they *spend* more.

MEANING EXPRESSED	*IF* CLAUSE	INDEPENDENT CLAUSE
2. Prediction/ possibility	Simple present	*will, can, should, might* + base form

▶ If you *turn* left here, you *will end up* in Mississippi.

3. Speculation   Simple past *or*   *would, could,*
   about   subjunctive   *should, might* +
   present or   *were*   base form
   future

▶ If he *had* a **cell phone, he** *would use* **it.**

▶ If she *were* **my lawyer, I** *might win* **the case.**

---

4. Speculation   Past perfect   *would have*   ⎫
   about past   (*had* + past   *could have*   ⎬ + past
                  participle)   *should have* ⎭ participle
                                  might have

▶ If they *had saved* **the diaries, they** *could have sold*
  them.

NOTE: In standard written English, use *would* only in the independent clause, not in the conditional clause. However, *would* occurs frequently in the conditional clause in speech and informal use.

                            showed
▶ **If the fish fry committee** ~~would show~~ **more initiative,**
  more people might attend the events.

         had
▶ **If I** ~~would have~~ **heard their answer, I would have**
  been angry.

Wishes   For a present wish—about something that has not happened and is therefore hypothetical and imaginary—use the past tense or the subjunctive *were* in the dependent clause. For a wish about the past, use the past perfect: *had* + past participle.

A WISH ABOUT THE PRESENT

▶ **I wish I** *had* **your attitude.**

▶ **I wish that Shakespeare** *were* **still alive.**

▶ Some of us wish that the strike *had* never *occurred.*

▶ He wishes that he *had bought* a lottery ticket.

Requests, demands, and recommendations After certain verbs, such as *request, command, insist, demand, move* (in the sense of "propose"), *propose,* and *urge,* use the base form of the verb, regardless of the person and number of the subject.

▶ I suggest that this rule *be* changed.

▶ He insisted that she *hand in* the report.

22g Passive voice

In the active voice, the grammatical subject is the doer of the action, and the sentence gives a straightforward display of "who is doing what." The passive voice tells what *is done to* the subject of the sentence. The person or thing doing the action may or may not be mentioned but is always implied: "My car was repaired" (by somebody at the garage).

ACTIVE

```
      ┌── subject ──┐   active voice verb   ┌── direct object ──┐
▶ Alice Walker          wrote         The Color Purple.
```

PASSIVE

```
                              passive voice
      ┌──── subject ────┐   ┌── verb ──┐   ┌── doer or agent ──┐
▶ The Color Purple   was written   by Alice Walker.
```

To form the passive voice, use a form of the verb *be* followed by a past participle. Do not overuse the passive voice. A general rule is to use the passive voice only when the doer in your sentence is unknown or is unimportant or when you want to keep subjects consistent (see 16a).

▶ The puppies are rare. Four of them *will be sold* to a breeder.

Use the passive voice *only* with verbs that are transitive in English. Intransitive verbs such as *happen* and *occur* are not used in the passive voice.

▶ The ceremony ~~was~~ happened yesterday. ∎

23 Subject-Verb Agreement

In standard English, singular subjects take singular verbs, and plural subjects take plural verbs.

23a Basic principles

When you use the present tense, the subject and verb must agree in person (first, second, or third) and number (singular or plural). The ending -s is added to nouns and verbs in English, but in very different contexts.

KEY POINTS

Two Key Points about Agreement

1. Follow the *one -s rule*. You can either put an -s on the noun to make it plural or put an -s on the verb to make it singular (note the irregular forms *is* and *has*). An -s added to both subject and verb is not standard English.

FAULTY
AGREEMENT   **My friends comes over every Saturday.**

POSSIBLE   **My friend comes over every Saturday.**
REVISIONS   (one friend)

              My friends come over every Saturday.
              (more than one)

2. Do not drop a necessary -s.

   ▶ His sister wear*s* gold jewelry.

   ▶ The book on my desk describe*s* life in Tahiti.

23b Words between subject and verb

When words come between the subject and the verb, find the verb and ask *Who?* or *What?* about it to determine exactly what the subject is. Ignore any intervening words.

▶ **Her collection of baseball cards is much admired.**

[What is admired? The subject, *collection*, is singular.]

▶ **The government's proposals about preserving the environment cause controversy.**

[What things cause controversy? The subject, *proposals*, is plural.]

Do not be confused by intervening words ending in *-s*, such as *always* and *sometimes*. The *-s* ending still must appear on a present tense verb if the subject is singular.

▶ **His assistant always make̬ mistakes.**

                             ^s

Phrases introduced by *as well as, along with,* and *in addition to* that come between the subject and the verb do not change the number of the verb.

▶ **His daughter, as well as his two sons, want̬ him to move nearby.**

                                           ^s

23c Subject after verb

When the subject comes after the verb in the sentence, the subject and verb must still agree.

1. *Questions* In a question, the auxiliary verb agrees with the subject, which follows the verb.

   ▶ *Does* **the editor agree to the changes?**

                 —————— plural subject ——————
   ▶ *Do* **the editor and the production manager agree to them?**

2. *Initial* **here** *or* **there** When a sentence begins with *here* or *there*, the verb agrees with the subject, which follows the verb.

   ▶ **There** *is* **a reason to rejoice.**

   ▶ **There** *are* **many reasons to rejoice.**

       It does not follow the same pattern as *here* and *there*. Sentences beginning with *it* always take a singular verb.

   ▶ **It** *is* **hundreds of miles away.** ■

3. *Inverted order* When a sentence begins not with the subject but with a phrase preceding the verb, the verb still agrees with the subject, which follows it.

┌── prepositional phrase ──┐ plural verb ┌── plural subject ──┐
▶ **In front of the library sit two stone lions.**

23d Tricky singular subjects

1. **Each** *and* every *Each* and *every* may seem to indicate more than one, but grammatically they are singular words, used with a singular verb.

   ▶ **Each of the cakes** *has* **a different frosting.**

   ▶ **Every conceivable type of problem** *arises* **in the first few weeks.**

2. **-ing** *words* With a noun formed from an *-ing* verb (called a *gerund*) as a subject, always use a singular verb form.

   ▶ **Playing the piano in front of a crowd** *causes* **anxiety.**

3. *Singular nouns ending in* -s Some nouns end in *-s* (*news, politics, economics, physics, mathematics, statistics*), but they are not plural. Use them with a singular verb.

   ▶ **Politics** *is* **dirty business.**

4. *Phrases of time, money, and weight* When the subject is regarded as one unit, use a singular verb.

   ▶ **Five hundred dollars** *is* **too much to pay.**

5. *Uncountable nouns* An uncountable noun (such as *furniture, money, equipment, food, advice, happiness, honesty, information, knowledge*) encompasses all the items in its class. An uncountable noun does not have a plural form and is always followed by a singular verb (**34a**, ESL).

   ▶ **The information found in the newspapers** *is* **not always accurate.**

6. **One of** *One of* is followed by a plural noun and a singular verb form.

   ▶ *One of* **her friends** *loves* **to tango.**

7. **The number of** The phrase *the number of* is followed by a plural noun (the object of the preposition *of*) and a singular verb form.

   ▶ **The number of reasons** *is* **growing.**

   However, with *a number of,* meaning "several," use a plural verb.

   ▶ **A number of reasons** *are* **listed in the letter.**

8. *A title of a work or a word used to refer to the word itself* Use a singular verb with a title of a work or a word used to refer to the word itself.

   ▶ <u>Cats</u> *was* **entertaining.**

   ▶ **In her story, the word** <u>yikes</u> *appears* **five times.**

23e Collective nouns

Generally, use a singular verb form with a collective noun like *class, government, family, jury, committee, group, couple,* or *team.*

▶ **My family** *goes* **on vacation every year.**

A plural verb form can be used, though, if you wish to emphasize differences among the individuals or if the group is thought of as individuals.

▶ **The jury** *are* **from a variety of backgrounds.**

You can also avoid the issue by revising the sentence.

▶ **The members of the jury** *are* **from a variety of backgrounds.**

However, with collective nouns like *police, poor, elderly,* and *young,* always use plural verbs.

▶ **The elderly** *deserve* **our respect.**

23f Compound subjects

With and   When a subject has two or more parts joined by *and*, treat the subject as plural and use a plural verb form.

▶ **His daughter and his son** *want* **him to move to Florida.**

However, if the two joined parts refer to a single person or thing, use a singular verb.

▶ **The restaurant's chef and owner** *makes* **good fajitas.**

With each *or* every   When *each* or *every* is used with a subject that has two or more parts joined by *and*, use a singular verb.

▶ **Every toy and game** *has* **to be put away.**
▶ **Each plate and glass** *looks* **new.**

With or *or* nor   With compound subjects joined by *or* or *nor*, the verb agrees with the part of the subject nearer to it.

▶ **Her sister or her parents** *plan* **to visit her next week.**
▶ **Neither her parents nor her sister** *drives* **a station wagon.**

23g Indefinite pronouns

Use a singular verb with the following indefinite pronoun subjects.

> someone, somebody, something
> anyone, anybody, anything
> no one, nobody, nothing
> everyone, everybody, everything
> each, either, neither, one

▶ **Neither of his parents** *knows* **where he is.**
▶ **Someone** *has* **been sitting in my chair.**
▶ **Each computer** *has* **a modem.**
▶ **Everyone** *agrees* **with you.**

For agreement with *one of*, see **23d**, item 6.

23h Quantity words

Quantity words can be used alone or to modify a noun. Some are singular; some are plural; some can be used to indicate either singular or plural, depending on the noun they refer to.

WORDS EXPRESSING QUANTITY	
WITH SINGULAR NOUNS AND VERBS	WITH PLURAL NOUNS AND VERBS
much	many
(a) little	(a) few (see p. 188)
a great deal (of)	several
a large amount (of)	a large number (of)
less	fewer
another	both

▶ Much *has* been accomplished.

▶ Much progress still *needs* to be made.

▶ Many *have* gained from the recent stock market rise.

▶ Many activities *let* everyone participate.

▶ Few of his fans *are* buying his recent book.

You will see and hear *less* used in place of *fewer,* but in formal writing, use only *fewer* to refer to a plural word.

▶ More *movies* have been made this year than last, but *fewer have* made money.

The following quantity words can be used with both singular and plural nouns and verbs: *all, any, half (of), more, most, no, none, other, part (of), some.*

▶ You gave me some information. More *is* necessary.

▶ You gave me some facts. More *are* needed.

23i Relative clauses (*who, which, that*)

Determine subject-verb agreement within a relative (adjective) clause by asking whether the antecedent of a subject relative pronoun (*who, which, that*) is singular or plural.

▶ The book that *has been* at the top of the bestseller list for weeks gives advice about health. [*Book* is the antecedent of *that*.]

▶ The books that *have been* near the top of the bestseller list for a few weeks give advice about making money.

[*Books* is the antecedent of *that*.]

For more on relative pronouns, see **24e**.

24 Pronouns

A pronoun is a word that refers to or replaces a noun.

▶ Jack's hair is so long that *it* hangs over *his* collar.

[*It* refers to *hair*; *his* refers to *Jack*.]

24a Personal pronouns

Personal pronouns have different forms to express person (first, second, or third), number (singular or plural), and function in a clause (case).

KEY POINTS

Forms of Personal Pronouns

	SUBJECT	OBJECT	POSSESSIVE (BEFORE A NOUN)	POSSESSIVE (WITH NO FOLLOWING NOUN)
First person singular	I	me	my	mine
First person plural	we	us	our	ours
Second person singular and plural	you	you	your	yours
Third person singular	he	him	his	his
	she	her	her	hers
	it	it	its	its (rare)
Third person plural	they	them	their	theirs

After a linking verb   Use the subject form of the pronoun after a linking verb, such as *be*.

he
▶ **Sam confessed that the cause of trouble was ~~him~~.**

[Many would choose to revise this sentence to sound less formal: "Sam confessed that he was the cause of the trouble."]

With an infinitive   Use an object pronoun after a verb used with an infinitive. When a sentence has only one object, this principle is easy to apply.

▶ **The dean wanted *him* to lead the procession.**

Difficulties occur with compound objects.

him and me
▶ **The dean wanted ~~he and I~~ to lead the procession.**

In a compound subject or object with and: **I** *or* me; he *or* him?   To decide which pronoun form to use with a compound subject or object, mentally recast the sentence with only the pronoun in the subject or object position.

I
▶ **Jenny and ~~me~~ went to the movies.**

[If *Jenny* is dropped, you would say *I went to the movies*, not *me went to the movies*. Here you need the subject form, *I*.]

me
▶ **They told my brother and ~~I~~ to wait in line.**

[If *my brother* is dropped, you would say *They told me to wait in line*. You need the object form, *me*.]

After a preposition   After a preposition, use an object form.

me
▶ **Between you and ~~I~~, the company is in serious trouble.**

In appositive phrases   When using a pronoun in an appositive phrase (one that gives more specific information about a preceding noun), determine whether the noun that the pronoun refers to functions as subject or as object.

► The supervisor praised only two employees, Ramon

    me

and ~~I~~.

► Only two employees, Ramon and ~~me~~, received a
bonus.

    I

We or *us* before a noun   Use *us* when the noun phrase is
the direct object of a verb or preposition, *we* when it is the
subject.

    us

► The singer waved to ~~we~~ fans.

    We

► ~~Us~~ fans have decided to form a club.

In comparisons   In comparisons with *than* and *as*, decide
on the subject or object form of the pronoun by mentally
completing the comparison.

► She is certainly not more intelligent than I. [... than I
am.]

► Jack and Sally work together; Jack sees his boss more
than she. [... more than she does.]

► Jack and Sally work together; Jack sees his boss more
than her. [... more than he sees Sally.]

Possessive pronoun before an -ing *form*   Generally,
use a possessive pronoun before an *-ing* verb form used as a
noun (a *gerund*).

► We appreciate *your* participating in the auction.

► *Their* winning the marathon surprised us all.

    Sometimes, though, the *-ing* form is not used as a noun.
In that case, the pronoun preceding the *-ing* form should be
the object form.

► We saw *them* giving the runners foil wraps.

No apostrophe with possessive pronouns   Even
though possessive in meaning, the pronouns *yours, ours,
theirs, his,* and *hers* should never be used with an apostrophe.
Use an apostrophe only with the possessive form of a noun.

▶ That coat is *Maria's*.

▶ That is *her* coat.

▶ That coat is *hers*.

For the distinction between *its* and *it's*, see **27d**.

24b Clear reference

A pronoun refers to or replaces a noun, a noun phrase, or a pronoun already mentioned, known as its *antecedent*.

▶ Because the Canadian skater practiced daily, *she* won the championship. [*She* refers to *skater*.]

State a specific antecedent. Avoid using a pronoun such as *they*, *this*, or *it* without an explicit antecedent.

NO SPECIFIC ANTECEDENT	**When Rivera applied for a loan, they outlined the procedures.**
	[The sentence does not have a clear antecedent for the pronoun *they*.]
REVISION	**When Rivera applied for a loan, bank officials outlined the procedures.**

Do not make a pronoun refer to a possessive noun or to a noun within a prepositional phrase.

George Orwell
▶ In ~~George Orwell's~~ "Shooting an Elephant," ~~he~~ reports an incident that shows the evil effects of imperialism.

Avoid an ambiguous reference. Your readers should never be left wondering which *this*, *they*, or *it* is being discussed.

AMBIGUOUS REFERENCE	**He faced having to decide whether to move to California. This was not what he wanted to do.**
	[We do not know what *this* refers to: having to decide? moving to California?]
REVISION	**He faced having to decide whether to move to California. This decision was not one he wanted to make.**

24c Agreement with antecedent

A plural antecedent needs a plural pronoun; a singular antecedent needs a singular pronoun.

▶ Listeners heard *they* could win free tickets. The ninth caller learned *she* was the winner.

NOTE: Demonstrative pronouns *this* and *that* are singular. *These* and *those* are the plural forms.

A generalized (generic) antecedent   Generic nouns describe a class or type of person or object, such as *a student* meaning "all students." Do not use *they* to refer to a singular generic noun, and make sure that you use *he* and *she* without gender bias (18c).

FAULTY AGREEMENT	When *a student* is educated, *they* can go far in the world.
POSSIBLE REVISIONS	When *a student* is educated, *he or she* can go far in the world.
	When *students* are educated, *they* can go far in the world.

Often, a plural noun is preferable as it avoids clumsy repetition of *he or she*. See **18c**.

▶ We should judge ~~a person~~ by who ~~he or she is~~, not
  ^people   ^they are
by the color of ~~his or her~~ skin.
                 ^their

A collective noun   Refer to a collective noun like *class, family, jury, committee, couple,* or *team* with a singular pronoun.

▶ The committee has not yet completed *its* report.

However, when the members of the group named by the collective noun are considered to be acting individually, use a plural pronoun.

▶ The committee began to cast *their* ballots in a formal vote.

An indefinite pronoun   Indefinite pronouns, such as *one, each, either, neither, everyone, everybody, someone, somebody, something, anyone, anybody, anything, no one, nobody,* and *nothing,* are generally singular in form (**23g**). A singular antecedent needs a singular pronoun to refer to it. For many years, the prescribed form in standard English was *he,* as in sentences such as *Everyone needs his privacy* or *Each person needs his privacy.* Now, however, such usage is regarded as biased—*he or she* is clumsy, and *they,* while used often in informal writing, is regarded by many as not accurate. Use a plural noun and pronoun instead.

NOT APPROPRIATE *Everyone* picked up *his* [*his or her; their*] **marbles and went home.**

REVISED *The children* picked up *their* **marbles and went home.**

24d Appropriate use of *you*

In writing, do not use *you* for general reference, to mean "people generally." Use *you* only to address the reader directly, as in "If you turn to the table on page ten, you will find...."

▶ While growing up, ~~you~~ teenagers face arguments with ~~your~~ their parents.

24e *Who, whom, which, that*

When to use who, which, *or* that Use *who* (or *whom*) to refer to human beings; use *which* or *that* to refer to animals, objects, or concepts.

▶ The teacher ~~which~~ who taught me algebra was strict.

When to use who *or* whom *Whom* is an object pronoun. You will often hear and read *who* in its place, but some readers prefer the standard form.

▶ Whom [informal *who*] did Romeo love?

Whom used as a relative pronoun can often be omitted.

▶ The players [whom] the team honored invited everyone to the party.

Do not use *whom* in place of *who:*

who
▶ The dancer ~~whom~~ is doing the tango is a scientist.

When to use which *or* that   Generally, use *that* rather than *which* in restrictive clauses (ones that provide necessary rather than extra information—see **26c**). When *that* is the object of its clause, you can omit it. Use *which* when you provide extra information.

▶ The book [*that*] you gave me was fascinating.

▶ <u>War and Peace</u> , *which* you gave me, was fascinating.

 Note that *what* cannot be used as a relative pronoun.

that
▶ Everything ~~what~~ she does receives praise. ■

25 Adjectives and Adverbs

Adjectives describe, or modify, nouns or pronouns. They do not add *-s* or change form to reflect number or gender.

▶ He tried three *different* approaches.

Adverbs modify verbs, adjectives, and other adverbs, as well as whole clauses.

▶ She settled down *comfortably.*

25a Correct forms of adjectives and adverbs

Check your dictionary for information on adjective and adverb forms not covered here.

Adverb: adjective + -ly   Many adverbs are formed by adding *-ly* to an adjective: *intelligent/intelligently.* Sometimes when *-ly* is added, a spelling change occurs: *easy/easily.*

Adjectives ending in -ic   To form an adverb from an adjective ending in *-ic,* add *-ally (basic, basically; artistic, artistically),* with the exception of *public,* whose adverb form is *publicly.*

Irregular adverb forms   Certain other adjectives do not add -*ly* to form an adverb:

ADJECTIVE	ADVERB
good	well
fast	fast
hard	hard

▶ He is a *good* cook.   ▶ He *cooks* well.

NOTE: *Well* can also function as an adjective, meaning "healthy" or "satisfactory."

▶ A *well* baby smiles often.   ▶ She feels *well* today.

25b When to use adjectives and adverbs

In speech, adjectives (particularly *good, bad,* and *real*) are often used to modify verbs, adjectives, or adverbs. This is nonstandard usage.

        clearly   really well
▶ She speaks very ~~clear.~~   ▶ I sing ~~real good~~.

After linking verbs like *be, seem, appear,* and *become,* use an adjective (as a complement).

▶ She seems *pleasant.*

Some verbs, such as *appear, look, feel, smell,* and *taste,* are sometimes used as linking verbs, sometimes as action verbs. If the modifier tells about the subject, use an adjective. If the modifier tells about the action of the verb, not the subject, use an adverb.

ADJECTIVE	She looks *confident* in her new job.
ADVERB	She looks *confidently* at all the assembled partners.
ADJECTIVE	The steak smells *bad.*
ADVERB	The chef smelled the lobster *appreciatively.*

25c Compound adjectives

A compound adjective needs hyphens to connect its parts. Note the forms when a compound adjective is used:

hyphens, no noun plural endings, and *-ed* endings where necessary (see also **32b**).

▶ They have a *five-year-old* daughter. [Their daughter is five years old.]

▶ He is a *left-handed* pitcher. [He pitches with his left hand.]

Many compound adjectives use the *-ed* form: *flat-footed, barrel-chested, broad-shouldered, old-fashioned, well-dressed, left-handed.*

25d Avoiding double negatives

Although some languages and dialects allow more than one negative to emphasize an idea, standard English uses only one negative in a clause. Words like *hardly, scarcely,* and *barely* are considered negatives. The contraction *-n't* stands for the adverb *not.* Avoid double negatives.

DOUBLE NEGATIVE	**We do*n't* have *no* excuses.**
REVISED	**We do*n't* have any excuses.**
	We have *no* excuses.

DOUBLE NEGATIVE	**They ca*n't* *hardly* pay the rent.**
REVISED	**They can *hardly* pay the rent.**

25e Comparative and superlative forms

Adjectives and adverbs have *comparative* and *superlative* forms that are used for comparisons. Use the comparative form when comparing two items, people, places, or ideas; use the superlative form when comparing more than two.

SHORT ADJECTIVES		
	COMPARATIVE (COMPARING TWO)	SUPERLATIVE (COMPARING MORE THAN TWO)
short	shorter	shortest
pretty	prettier	prettiest
simple	simpler	simplest
fast	faster	fastest

LONG ADJECTIVES AND *-LY* ADVERBS		
	COMPARATIVE	SUPERLATIVE
intelligent	more intelligent	most intelligent
carefully	more carefully	most carefully

If you cannot decide whether to use an *-er/-est* form or *more/most*, consult a dictionary. If there is an *-er/-est* form, the dictionary will say so.

NOTE: Do not use the *-er* form with *more* or the *-est* form with *most*.

▶ The first poem was ~~more~~ better than the second.

▶ Boris is the ~~most~~ fittest person I know.

Irregular forms

	COMPARATIVE	SUPERLATIVE
good	better	best
bad	worse	worst
much/many	more	most
well	better	best
badly	worse	worst

25f Avoiding faulty and incomplete comparisons

Make sure that you state clearly what items you are comparing. Some faulty comparisons can give a reader the wrong idea.

                                                                does
▶ He likes the parrot better than his wife.

▶ Williams's poem gives a more objective depiction of
                                            's
the painting than Auden. [To compare Williams's poem with Auden's poem, you need to include an apostrophe; otherwise you compare a poem to the poet W. H. Auden.]

Part 6
Punctuation and Mechanics

26 Commas

A comma separates parts of a sentence; it does not separate one sentence from another. To determine whether to use a comma, follow the guidelines in the boxes in **26a** and **26b**.

Commas: yes

You will find variations in comma use, but the following guidelines are generally acceptable.

KEY POINTS

Commas: Yes

1. Between two independent clauses connected by a coordinating conjunction: *and, but, or, nor, so, for,* or *yet*

   ▶ He frowned, but she did not understand why he was worried.

   Comma use can be optional if the clauses are short.

   ▶ He offered to help and he did.

2. After a phrase or a dependent clause occurring before the subject of the independent clause

   ▶ After they had eaten, their mother arrived with ice cream for dessert.

   Note how omitting the comma can lead to a misreading.

3. Before and after extra (nonrestrictive) information inserted in a sentence ("extra commas with extra information"—see 26c)

   ▶ My father, a computer programmer, works late at night.

4. To set off transitional expressions

   ▶ The ending, however, is disappointing.

5. Between three or more items in a series

   ▶ She plays baseball, basketball, and golf.

6. Between adjectives that can also be connected with *and*

   ▶ We ate a delicious, well-prepared, and inexpensive meal.

7. To separate a direct quotation from a subject and verb

   ▶ "I intend to win an Oscar," she announced.

26b Commas: no

 KEY POINTS

Commas: No

1. Not separating subject and verb

   ▶ **The gorilla sitting in a corner of the cage stared at us.**

   (However, use two commas to set off any extra material inserted between subject and verb, as in item 3, in **26a**.)

2. Not before part of a compound structure that is not a complete independent clause

   ▶ **She won the trophy and accepted it graciously.**

3. Not *after* a coordinating conjunction (*and, but, or, nor, so, for, yet*) connecting two independent clauses, but *before* it

   ▶ **The movie tried to be engaging, but it failed.**

4. Not between two independent clauses without a coordinating conjunction (use either a period and a capital letter or a semicolon instead)

   ▶ **He won; she was delighted.**

5. Not separating an independent clause from a following dependent clause introduced by *after, before, because, if, since, unless, until,* or *when* (no comma, either before or after the subordinating conjunction)

   ▶ **She will continue working for the city until she has saved enough for graduate school.**

6. Not before a clause beginning with *that*

   ▶ **They warned us that the meeting would be difficult.**

   However, note that a comma can appear before a *that* clause when it is the second comma of a pair before and after inserted material: *He skates so fast, despite his size, that he will probably break the world record.*

7. Not before and after essential (restrictive) information (26c)

   ▶ **The player who scored the goal became a hero.**

8. Not between a verb and its object or complement

   ▶ **The best gifts are food and clothes.**

9. Not after *such as*

   ▶ **Popular fast-food items, such as hamburgers and hot dogs, tend to be high in cholesterol.**

■

26c Commas with extra (nonrestrictive) elements

Use commas to set off information inserted in a sentence when that information can be removed without changing the basic message. If the insertion comes in midsentence, it needs to be set off by a pair of commas.

▶ **She loves her car, a red Toyota.**

[The insert after the comma provides additional information about "her car."]

▶ **His dog, a big Labrador retriever, is afraid of mice.**

[If you read "His dog is afraid of mice," you would not necessarily need to know what type of dog he owns. The insert provides additional, not necessary, information.]

▶ **My boss, who is only twenty-five, has been promoted.**

[The independent clause "My boss has just been promoted" does not lead the reader to ask "Which boss?" The relative clause merely adds interesting information; it does not define or restrict the noun *boss*.]

▶ **His recent paintings, which are hanging in our local restaurant, show dogs in various disguises.**

[The clause introduced by *which* tells us an additional fact: that his recent paintings are in the restaurant.]

Do not use commas to set off essential information.

▶ **The people who live in the apartment above mine make too much noise.** [If you read only "The people make too much noise," you would ask "Which people?" The relative clause here restricts "the people" to a subgroup: Not all people make too much noise; those in the apartment above do.]

26d Special uses of commas

• Use a comma or commas to set off a phrase that modifies the whole sentence (an absolute phrase).

▶ **The audience looking on in amusement, the valedictorian blew kisses to all her favorite instructors.**

• Use a comma or commas to set off an inserted idea or a conversational tag (such as *yes, no, well,* or a direct address).

▶ **Yes, Joyce Maynard, like others before her, has produced a "tell-all" memoir.**

▶ **Whatever you build here, Mr. Trump, will cause controversy.**

• Use a comma to separate the day from the year in a date.

▶ **On May 14, 1998, the legendary singer Frank Sinatra died.** [Note, however, that no comma is used before the year in the alternate style for dates when the day precedes the month: 14 May 1998.]

• Use a comma (never a period) to divide numbers into thousands.

▶ **1,200** ▶ **515,000** ▶ **34,000,000**

No commas are necessary in years (1999), numbers in addresses (3501 East 10th Street), or page numbers (page 1002).

• Use commas around a person's title or degree.

▶ **Stephen L. Carter, Ph.D., gave the commencement speech.**

- Use a comma to separate the parts of an address.

  ▶ **Alice Walker was born in Eatonton, Georgia, in 1944.**

  However, do not use a comma before a ZIP code: Berkeley, CA 94704.

27 Apostrophes

Apostrophes are used to show a possessive relationship (*the government's plans*—the plans of the government, belonging to the government). They also signal omitted letters.

 Apostrophes: yes and no

 KEY POINTS

Apostrophe: Yes

1. Use -'s for the possessive form of all nouns except those already ending in plural -s: *student's, reporter's, women's.*
2. Use an apostrophe alone for the possessive form of plural nouns ending in -s: *students', reporters'.*
3. Use an apostrophe to indicate omitted letters in contracted forms, such as *didn't, they're, they'd.* However, some readers of formal academic writing may object to such contractions.
4. Use *it's* only for "it is" or "it has": *It's a good idea; it's been a long time.*

■

 KEY POINTS

Apostrophe: No

1. Do not use an apostrophe to form plurals of nouns: *big bargains, coming attractions.* See **27c** for rare exceptions.
2. Never use an apostrophe before an -s ending on a verb: *She likes him.*

(continued)

(continued)

3. Do not use an apostrophe with possessive pronouns *(hers, its, ours, yours, theirs): The house lost its roof.*

4. Do not use an apostrophe to form the plurals of names *(the Browns),* abbreviations *(VCRs),* and decades *(the 1990s).*

5. Do not use an apostrophe to indicate possession with names of buildings, items of furniture, and other objects; instead, use *of: the roof of the hotel, the back of the desk.* ■

27b Apostrophe + -*s* (-'*s*): special cases to show possession

More than one noun When you want to indicate separate ownership for two nouns in a sentence, make each one possessive.

▶ **Updike's and Roth's recent works have received glowing reviews.**

For joint ownership, use only one apostrophe: *Sam and Pat's house.*

Compound nouns Add the -'*s* to the last part.

▶ **my brother-in-law's car**

Singular words ending in -s Add -'*s* as usual for the possessive.

▶ **Thomas's toys**

However, when a singular word ending in -*s* has a -*z* pronunciation, an apostrophe alone is sometimes used: *Charles' mother.*

27c -'*s* for a plural form in two instances

1. Use -'*s* for the plural form of letters of the alphabet. Italicize (or underline) only the letter, not the plural ending.

▶ **Georges Perec wrote a novel with no *e*'s in it at all.**

2. Use -'s for the plural form of a word used to refer to the word itself. Italicize or underline the word used as a word, but do not italicize the -'s ending.

▶ **You have used too many *but*'s in that sentence.**

NOTE: With numbers and abbreviations, MLA guidelines recommend no apostrophe: *the 1900s, CDs, FAQs, B.A.s.* However, you will frequently find these used with -'s. Just be consistent in your usage.

27d *It's* and *its*

When deciding on *its* or *it's*, think about meaning. *It's* means *it is* or *it has*. *Its* means "belonging to it." If you intend *it is* or *it has*, you need the apostrophe. If not, use no apostrophe.

▶ **It's a good idea.**   ▶ **The committee took its time.**

28 Quotation Marks

Quotation marks indicate the beginning and end of a quotation or a title of a short work. The text between the quotation marks is marked off as the exact words that someone said, thought, or wrote.

28a Punctuation introducing and ending a quotation

• After an introductory verb, use a comma followed by a capital letter to introduce a direct quotation.

▶ **Calvin Trillin says, "As far as I'm concerned, *whom* is a word that was invented to make everyone sound like a butler."**   —"Whom Says So?"

• Use a colon after a complete sentence introducing a quotation and begin the quotation with a capital letter.

▶ **Woody Allen always makes us laugh even about serious issues like wealth and poverty: "Money is better than poverty, if only for financial reasons."**   —*Without Feathers*

When the quotation is integrated into the structure of your own sentence, use no special introductory punctuation other than the quotation marks.

> ▶ Phyllis Grosskurth comments that "anxiety over money was driving him over the brink."
>
> —*Byron*

- Put periods and commas inside quotation marks, even if these punctuation marks do not appear in the original quotation.

> ▶ When Rosovsky characterizes Bloom's ideas as "mind-boggling," he is not offering praise.
>
> —*The University*

However, in a documented paper, when you use parenthetical citations after a short quotation at the end of a sentence, put the period at the end of the citation, not within the quotation. See **8a** for long quotations.

> ▶ Geoffrey Wolff observes that when his father died there was nothing "to suggest that he had ever known another human being" **(11).**
>
> —*The Duke of Deception*

- Put question marks and exclamation points inside the quotation marks if they are part of the original source, with no additional period. When your sentence is a statement, do not use a comma or period in addition to a question mark or exclamation point.

> ▶ She asked, "Where's my mama?"

- Put a question mark, exclamation point, semicolon, or colon that belongs to your sentence outside the closing quotation marks. If your sentence contains punctuation that is your own, not part of the original quotation, do not include it within the quotation marks.

> ▶ The chapter focuses on this question: Who are "the new American dreamers"?

28b Quotation marks in dialogue

Do not add closing quotation marks until the speaker changes or you interrupt the quotation. Begin each new speaker's words on a new line.

▶ "I'm not going to work today," he announced to his son. "Why should I? My boss is away on vacation. And I have a headache."

"Honey, your boss is on the phone," his wife called from the bedroom.

If a quotation from one speaker continues for more than one paragraph, do not place closing quotation marks at the end of the first paragraph. However, open the new paragraph with quotation marks so that your readers realize that the quotation continues.

28c Double and single quotation marks

In American English, quotations are enclosed in double quotation marks. Single quotation marks are used for a quotation inside a quotation. (British English usage is different.)

▶ Margaret announced, "I have read 'The Lottery' already."

28d Quotation marks with titles of short works

Enclose in quotation marks the title of a short work you refer to, such as a short story, poem, article, song, TV program (not a series), or book chapter.

▶ Ishmael Reed's essay "America: The Multinational Society" begins with an illuminating quotation.

28e When not to use quotation marks

- Do not use quotation marks with indirect quotations.

  ▶ One woman I interviewed said that her husband argued like a lawyer.

- Do not use quotation marks with clichés, slang, or trite expressions. Instead, avoid the cliché, slang, or trite expression. See also **18a**, **18b**.

  involvement.
  ▶ All they want is ~~"a piece of the action."~~

- Do not use quotation marks with long indented quotations. In academic writing, when you use MLA style to quote more than three lines of poetry or four typed lines of prose, indent the whole passage one inch (or ten spaces) from the left margin. Do not include the quoted passage in quotation marks, but retain any internal quotation marks. See **8a** for an illustration.

- Do not use quotation marks around your own essay title. The only time to use quotation marks in your title is when you use a quotation or the title of a short work within your title. Otherwise, use no quotation marks around your own title.

> ▶ **The Benefits of Bilingual Education**

> ▶ **Charles Baxter's "Gryphon" as a Warning**

29 Other Punctuation Marks

29a Periods, question marks, and exclamation points

These three punctuation marks end a sentence. The Modern Language Association (MLA), in its list of Frequently Asked Questions (*http://www.mla.org/set_stl.htm*), recommends leaving one space after a punctuation mark at the end of a sentence, as in published works, but it also sees "nothing wrong with using two spaces after concluding punctuation marks" and advises you to consult your instructor. Many readers of typescript prefer two spaces between sentences. In a list of works cited, however, whether MLA or APA, leave only one space after each period in an entry.

Periods (.) A period is used to end a sentence or to signal an abbreviation: *Mr., B.A., U.S.* Periods are not used in names of government agencies or organizations indicated by initials, in acronyms (abbreviations pronounced as words), or in Internet abbreviations by initials: ACLU, FTP, IRS, NOW.

Question marks (?) A question mark signals a direct question.

> ▶ **What is he writing?**

Do not use a question mark with an indirect question (**36c**, ESL).

▶ **Nobody asked him what he was writing.**

Exclamation points (!) An exclamation point at the end of a sentence tells the reader that the writer considers this material amazing, surprising, or extraordinary. Avoid overuse, and never accompany an exclamation point with a period, comma, or question mark.

29b Semicolons

- Use a semicolon between two independent clauses to avoid a run-on sentence or a comma splice.

    Use a semicolon instead of a period when the ideas in two independent clauses are very closely connected, but do not use a capital letter to begin a clause after a semicolon.

    ▶ **Biography tells us about the subject; biographers also tell us about themselves.**

    Semicolons are often used when the second independent clause contains a transitional expression like *however, moreover, in fact, nevertheless, above all, or therefore* (see **16b** for more on transitional expressions).

    ▶ **The results of the study support the hypothesis; however, further research with a variety of tasks is necessary.**

- Use semicolons to separate items in a list containing internal commas.

    Items in a list are usually separated by commas. However, to avoid ambiguity in a list in which additional internal commas appear, use semicolons to separate the items.

    ▶ **When I cleaned out the refrigerator, I found a chocolate cake, half-eaten; some canned tomato paste, which had a blue fungus growing on the top; and some possibly edible meat loaf.**

- Do not use semicolons interchangeably with colons. A colon, not a semicolon, is used to introduce a list or an explanation.

  ▶ They contributed a great deal of food⁚salad, chili, and dessert.

- Do not use a semicolon if a phrase or a dependent clause precedes it, even if that element is long. Using a semicolon produces a fragment. Use a comma instead.

  ▶ Because the training period was so long and arduous for all the players⁚the manager allowed one visit by family and friends.

29c Colons

A colon (:) follows an independent clause and introduces information that balances or explains that clause. A colon says to a reader, "What comes next will tell you more about what you have just read."

- Use a colon after an independent clause to introduce a list, a quotation, an explanation, or a rule.

  ▶ The students included three pieces of writing in their portfolios: a narrative, an argument, and a documented paper.

  ▶ Oscar Wilde makes the point well: "The real schools should be the streets."

Note that a capital letter is often used when an explanatory sentence or a rule follows a colon.

  ▶ The author has performed a remarkable feat: She has maintained suspense to the last page.

  ▶ The main principle of public speaking is simple: Look at the audience.

- Use a colon in salutations, in letters and memos, precise time notations, titles, and biblical citations.

Dear Chancellor Witkin: To: The Chancellor

7:20 P.M.   Genesis 37:31–35.
Lessons: A Memoir   (Here, a period can also be
                           used, in place of the colon.)

- Do not use a colon directly after a verb (such as a form of *be* or *include*), a preposition, or expressions such as *for example*, *especially*, and *such as*.

  ▶ **The book includes a preface, an introduction, an appendix, and an index.**

  ▶ **They packed many different items for the picnic, such as taco chips, salsa, bean salad, pita bread, and egg rolls.**

  ▶ **His taste is so varied that his living room includes, for example, antiques, modern art, and art deco lighting fixtures.**

29d Dashes, parentheses, and slashes

Dashes (—) Dashes set off material that is inserted into a sentence. Type two hyphens with no extra space before, after, or between them.

▶ **Armed with one weapon—his wit—he set off.**

Commas can sometimes be used to set off inserted material, too, but when the insertion itself contains commas, dashes are preferable.

▶ **The contents of his closet—torn jeans, frayed jackets and suits shiny on the seat and elbows—made him reassess his priorities.**

Parentheses Parentheses mark an aside or some supplementary information.

▶ **Chuck Yeager's feat (the breaking of the sound barrier) led to increased competition in the space industry.**

Slashes (/) Slashes are used to separate fewer than four lines of poetry quoted within your own text. For quoting four or more lines of poetry, see **8a**.

▶ **Philip Larkin asks a question that many of us relate to: "Why should I let the toad *work* / Squat on my life?"**

Slashes are also used to designate word options, such as *and/or* and *he/she*. Do not overuse these options.

29e Brackets and ellipsis dots

Square brackets ([ ]) Square brackets indicate inserted, changed, or omitted material within a quotation. Insert only words or parts of words that help the quotation fit into your sentence grammatically or that offer necessary explanation.

▶ Maxine Hong Kingston agrees with reviewer Diane Johnson that the memoir form "can neither [be] dismiss[ed] as fiction nor quarrel[ed] with as fact."

Angle brackets (< >) Angle brackets are used to enclose e-mail addresses and URLs (Web addresses), particularly in an MLA-style works cited list. See **10c**, items 32–45.

Ellipsis dots (. . .) Ellipsis dots indicate that you have omitted material from a quotation. Use three ellipsis dots enclosed in square brackets (MLA style) when you omit material from the middle of a quotation. Do not use ellipsis dots at the beginning or end of a quotation unless the omission of part of a sentence occurs at the beginning or end of your own sentence.

▶ Ruth Sidel reports that the women in her interviews "have a commitment to career [. . .] and to independence" (27).

When the omitted material falls at the end of a quoted sentence, put a period after the three ellipsis dots inside square brackets, making four dots in all. (For the conventions of documentation, see Sections 10–13.)

▶ Ruth Sidel reports that some women "have a commitment to career, to material well-being, to success, and to independence [. . .]. In short, they want their piece of the American Dream" (27).

To omit material at the end of a quoted sentence when the omission coincides with the end of your own sentence, use three dots within square brackets and place the sentence period after the parenthetical reference to the source.

▶ Ruth Sidel reports that some women "have a commitment to career [. . .] "(27).

When you omit one line or more of poetry, replace the omitted material with a line of dots within square brackets.

▶ **This poem is for the hunger of my mother**
[. . . . .]
who read the Blackwell's
catalogue like a menu of delights
—Aurora Levins Morales, *Class Poem*

30 Italics and Underlining

Use italics or underlining to highlight a word, phrase, or title. Most word processing programs offer italic type. Usually, though, in manuscript form, underlining is more distinctive and therefore often preferred, particularly in bibliographical lists of references and in material to be graded or typeset. For underlining when writing online, see **33b**.

▶ **Woolf's *Orlando* was written for Vita Sackville-West.**

▶ **In The Psychology of Time , we learn about perceptions of filled and empty time.**

30a Italicize or underline titles of long, whole works.

Italicize or underline the titles of works published as whole works: books, magazines, newspapers, plays, films, TV series, long poems, musical compositions, software programs, and works of art.

▶ **The Sun Also Rises** ▶ *Seinfeld*

▶ *Newsweek* ▶ **Mona Lisa**

Do not italicize or underline the Bible, books of the Bible (Genesis, Psalms), or the Koran, or documents such as the Declaration of Independence and the Constitution.

Do not italicize or underline titles of short works, including titles of your own essays. For short works not published separately, such as poems, short stories, essays, and articles, use quotation marks (**28d**).

▶ **"The Office"** [short story]

▶ **"Kubla Khan"** [poem]

30b Italicize or underline letters, figures, and words as words.

▶ The sign had a large <u>P</u> in black marker.

▶ *Zarf* is a useful word for some board games.

31 Capitals, Abbreviations, and Numbers

Use the following guidelines for capitalizing words.

31a Capitals

- Capitalize proper nouns and adjectives. Use capitals with the names of specific people, places, things, languages, and nationalities: Albert Einstein, Hungary, the Milky Way, Golden Gate Park, the Adirondacks, the Roosevelt Memorial, Wednesday, March, the Fourth of July, the Red Cross, University of Texas, Department of English, the Civil War, the Renaissance, Buddhism, Islam, the Torah, the Koran (or the Qu'ran), the Navajo, Greece, Greek, Spain, Spaniards, Spanish, Kleenex, the USS *Kearsage*.

  NOTE: Do not capitalize general classes or types of people, places, things, or ideas: *government, jury, mall, prairie, utopia, traffic, court, french fries, the twentieth century, goodness, reason.* For capital letters in online writing, see **33c**.

- Capitalize a title before a person's name.

  ▶ **The reporter interviewed Senator Thompson.**

  Do not use a capital when a title is not attached to a person.

  ▶ **Each state elects two senators.**

- Capitalize major words in titles. In titles of published books, journals, magazines, essays, articles, films, poems, and songs, use a capital letter for all words except articles *(the, a, an)*, coordinating conjunctions *(and, but, or, nor, so, for, yet)*, *to* in an infinitive *(to stay)*, and prepositions unless they begin or end a title or subtitle.

  ▶ **"Wrestling with the Angel: A Memoir"**

- Capitalize the first word of a quoted sentence when you introduce it with a complete sentence of your own.

  ▶ **Quindlen says, "This is a story about a name," and thus tells us the topic of her article.**

However, do not capitalize when you merge a quotation into your own sentence:

  ▶ **When Quindlen says that she is writing "a story about a name," she is telling us the topic of her article.**

For capital letters after colons, see **29c**.

31b Abbreviations

Use only the following types of abbreviations. Do not abbreviate words to save time and space. For example, write *through* and not *thru*, *night* and not *nite*.

- Abbreviate titles used with people's names. The following abbreviated titles appear before names: *Mr.*, *Ms.*, *Mrs.*, *Prof.*, *Dr.*, *Gen.*, and *Sen.* Note that *Miss* is not an abbreviation. The following abbreviated titles appear after names: *Sr.*, *Jr.*, *Ph.D.*, *M.D.*, *B.A.*, and *D.D.S.* Do not use a title both before and after a name.

  ▶ **Dr. Benjamin Spock**   ▶ **Benjamin Spock, M.D.**

- Do not abbreviate a title not attached to a name.

  doctor
  ▶ **He went to the ~~dr.~~ twice last week.**

- Abbreviate names of familiar institutions (UCLA, YMCA), countries (U.S.A.), examinations (SAT), diplomas (GED), people (FDR), and objects (VCR). If you use a specialized abbreviation, first use the term in full with the abbreviation in parentheses; then use the abbreviation. See **29a** for more on periods and abbreviations.

  ▶ **The Graduate Record Examination (GRE) is required by many graduate schools. GRE preparation is therefore big business.**

For the plural of an abbreviation, just add *-s: VCRs.*

- Abbreviate terms used with numbers. Use the abbreviations B.C., A.D., A.M., P.M., *$*, *mph*, *wpm*, *mg*, *kg*, and other units of measure only when they occur with specific numbers.

► **35 B.C.**　[meaning "before Christ," now often replaced with B.C.E., "before the common era"]

► **A.D. 1776**　[*anno domini*, "in the year of the Lord," now often replaced with C.E., "common era," used after the date: 1776 C.E.]

► **2:00 A.M. or 2:00 a.m.** [*ante meridiem*, Latin for "before midday"]

• But do not use the abbreviations B.C., A.D., A.M., P.M., $, *mph, wpm, mg, kg,* and other units of measure when no number is attached to them.

　　　　　　　　　　afternoon.
► **They arrived late in the p.m.**

• Abbreviate common Latin terms, such as *etc., e.g.,* and *N.B.,* but only in notes, parentheses, and source citations, not in the body of your text.

For abbreviations commonly used when writing online, see **33d.**

31c Numbers

In the humanities and in business letters, do the following:

Use words for numbers consisting of not more than two words and for fractions (*nineteen, fifty-six, two hundred, one-half*).

Use figures for longer numbers (*326; 5,625*).

Use a combination of words and figures for numbers over a million (*45 million*).

In scientific and technical writing, follow these guidelines:

Write all numbers above nine as figures.

Write numbers below ten as figures only when they show precise measurement, as when they are grouped and compared with other larger numbers (*5 of the 39 participants*), or when they precede a unit of measurement (*6 cm*), indicate a mathematical function *(8%; 0.4)*, or represent a specific time, date, age, score, or number in a series.

Write fractions as words.

Spell out numbers that occur at the beginning of a sentence.

▶ **One hundred twenty-five members voted for the new bylaws.**

▶ **Six thousand fans have already bought tickets.**

Even after plural numbers, the singular form of *hundred, thousand,* and *million* is used. Add a plural *-s* only when there is no preceding number: Hundreds *of books were damaged in the flood.* Five hundred *books were damaged in the flood.* ■

In nonscientific writing, use figures with the following:

Time and dates	6 P.M. on 31 May 1995
Decimals	20.89
Statistics	median score 35
Addresses	16 East 93rd Street
Chapters, pages, scenes, lines	Chapter 5, page 97
Abbreviations or symbols	6°C, for temperature Celsius, $21, 6'7"
Scores	The Knicks won 89–85.

For percentages and money, use the figure and symbol *(75%, $24.67)*, or spell out the expression if it is fewer than four words *(seventy-five percent, twenty-four dollars)*.

Use *-s*, not *-'s*, for the plural form of figures: *in the 1980s, 700s in the SATs.*

32 Hyphens

For the use of hyphens online, see **33c**.

32a Hyphens with prefixes

Many words with prefixes are written as one word without a hyphen: *cooperate, multilingual, unnatural.* Others, especially those beginning with a vowel sound, need a hyphen:

all-inclusive, self-indulgent. When the main word is a number or a proper noun, always use a hyphen: *all-American, post-1990.* If you are unsure about whether to use a hyphen, check a dictionary.

32b Hyphens with compound nouns and adjectives

Some compound words are written as one word without a hyphen (*toothbrush*), others as two words (*coffee shop*), and still others with one or more hyphens (*father-in-law*). Always check an up-to-date dictionary.

Use a hyphen with compound adjectives preceding a noun: *a well-organized party, a law-abiding citizen, a ten-page essay.* When the description follows the noun, no hyphen is necessary: *The party was well organized. Most citizens try to be law abiding. The essay was ten pages long.*

Do not use a hyphen between an *-ly* adverb and an adjective or after an adjective in its comparative (*-er*) or superlative (*-est*) form: *a tightly fitting suit, a sweeter sounding melody.*

32c Hyphens with numbers

Use hyphens with two-word numbers between twenty and ninety-nine whenever the numbers are spelled out: *Twenty-two applicants arrived early in the morning.* Also use a hyphen with spelled-out fractions—*two-thirds of a cup.*

32d Hyphens to split words at the end of a line

 Most word processors either automatically hyphenate words or automatically wrap words around to the next line. Choose the latter option to avoid the strange and unacceptable word division that can sometimes appear with automatic hyphenation. ■

Basic rules of hyphenation

1. Never hyphenate a word pronounced as one syllable.
2. Adjust hyphenation (or do not hyphenate) if only one letter remains at the end of a line or one or two letters appear at the beginning of a line.
3. Hyphenate only at syllable breaks or at a prefix or suffix.

4. Check hyphenation with double consonants. If a suffix has been added to a word ending in a double consonant, do not split the double consonant.

5. If a double consonant is formed only when a suffix is added, split the double consonant.

ERROR	REVISED
heal- th	health
watch- ed	watched
i- dea	idea
remonstrat- ed	remon- strated
merrim- ent	merri- ment
succes- sful	success- ful
dro- pping	drop- ping

33 Online Guidelines

33a Punctuation in URLs

Punctuation marks communicate essential information in Web site addresses (Uniform Resource Locators, or URLs) and in e-mail addresses. Make careful note of what the marks are and where they occur. Be sure to include all marks when you write addresses, and if you need to spread a URL over more than one line, split it after a slash (MLA style) or before a punctuation mark. Do not split the protocol (*http://*).

33b Underscoring, underlining, and italics online

In World Wide Web pages, in e-mail, and in HTML (hypertext markup language), underlining indicates a link to a new site, so underlining may not be available for other uses. When you write online, use italics to indicate titles and other underlined expressions. The single underscore mark is often used in place of italics and underlining in e-mail.

▶ **Just read Joyce's _Ulysses_ to get a flavor of Dublin.**

When you write a hard copy (paper) text, enclose URLs and e-mail addresses in angle brackets (< >), or italicize them. When you write online or prepare a works cited list in MLA style, enclose URLs in angle brackets.

33c Capitals and hyphens online

Lowercase and uppercase (capital) letters are significant in e-mail addresses and URLs (the technical term is *case-sensitive*), so keep careful records of which are used. If you get it wrong, you will be unable to make a connection. Similarly, many names of systems and search engines have specialized capitalization (the Internet, the World Wide Web, *MetaCrawler, AltaVista*). Follow the conventions.

Avoid using capitalized text (the whole text, not just initial letters) in e-mail communications and electronic discussion groups. In both places, the prolonged use of capital letters for communicating a message is regarded as "shouting," something that will offend your readers.

E-mail addresses sometimes include hyphens, so never add a hyphen to indicate that you have split an address between lines. If an e-mail address includes a hyphen, do not break the line at a hyphen—a reader will not know whether the hyphen is part of the address or not.

33d Asterisks, angle brackets, and abbreviations online

Asterisks (*) Many e-mail providers do not support text features such as italics or underlining; in such cases, use asterisks before and after a word or phrase for emphasis.

▶ They were *decidedly* antagonistic.

Angle brackets (< >) Use angle brackets to enclose e-mail and Web addresses.

▶ The Modern Language Association, whose Web site is at <http://www.mla.org>, provides examples of documenting Web sources.

Abbreviations Many abbreviations in the electronic world have now become standard fare: CD-ROM, RAM, PIN, and more. In addition, the informal world of online communication leads to informal abbreviations, at least in personal e-mail messages. Abbreviations such as BTW (by the way) and TTYTT (to tell you the truth) are used in e-mail but never appear in more formal written communication. See also **3c** for more on writing online.

Part 7

For Multilingual/ ESL Writers

Part 7 For Multilingual/ESL Writers

If English is not your native language, you will probably make some errors as you write, especially when you are grappling with new subject matter and difficult topics. For a guide to the specific types of errors commonly made by speakers of different languages, visit our Web site at <http://www.hmco.com/college> (click on English, then on the *Keys for Writers* site). This Web site also provides you with links to sites specifically designed for multilingual students.

---

34 *A, An,* and *The*

To decide whether to use *a, an, the,* or no article at all before a noun, first determine the type of noun you have.

34a What you need to know about nouns

Nouns fall into two categories.

Proper nouns   A proper noun names a unique person, place, or object and begins with a capital letter: *Walt Whitman, Lake Superior, Grand Canyon, Vietnam Veterans Memorial.*

Common nouns   A common noun does not name a unique person, place, object, or idea: *bicycle, furniture, plan, daughter, home, happiness.* Common nouns can be further categorized into two types, countable and uncountable:

- A *countable noun* can have a number before it (*one*, *two*, and so on); it has a plural form. Countable nouns frequently add *-s* to indicate the plural: *picture, pictures; plan, plans.* Singular countable nouns can be used after *a, an, the, this, that, each, every.* Plural countable nouns can be used after *the, these, those, many, a few, both, all, some, several.*

- An *uncountable noun* has no plural form: *furniture, equipment, advice, information.* Uncountable nouns can be used after *the, this, that, much, some, any, no, a little, a great deal of,* or a possessive such as *my* or *their.* They can never be used after a number or a plural quantity word such as *several* or *many.* Never use an uncountable noun after *a* or *an.*

▶ **My country has ∤ lovely scenery.**

NOTE: You can use an uncountable noun in a countable sense—that is, indicate a quantity of it—by adding a word or phrase that indicates quantity, but the noun itself always remains singular: three pieces of *furniture*, two bits of *information*, many pieces of *advice*.

Some nouns can be countable in one context and uncountable in another.

▶ **He loves *chocolate*.**

[All chocolate, applies to the class: uncountable]

▶ **She gave him *a chocolate*.**

[One piece of candy from a box: countable]

Articles: four basic questions

Ask four basic questions about a noun to decide whether to use an article and, if so, which article to use.

KEY POINTS

Articles at a Glance: Four Basic Questions

1. PROPER OR COMMON NOUN?
   ↓

   Singular: no
     article (zero article)
   Plural: *the*

(continued)

(continued)

2. SPECIFIC OR NONSPECIFIC REFERENCE?
↓

the (see **34d**)

3. UNCOUNTABLE OR COUNTABLE NOUN?
↓

no article or
some, much, etc.

4. PLURAL OR SINGULAR?
↓
no article or
some, many, etc.

a/an

Using the questions: a sample Answering the four questions can help you decide which article, if any, to use with the noun *jacket* in the following sentence:

▶ **The motorcyclist I saw on the street was carrying** ___?___ **jacket and wearing black leather pants.** article

1. *Jacket* is a common noun.
2. *Jacket* is not identified in the text as one specific jacket in the same way that *motorcyclist* is (the one the writer saw on the street).
3. *Jacket* is a countable noun.
4. *Jacket* is singular and begins with a consonant sound (*a* is used before a consonant sound, *an* before a vowel sound as in *an egg, an honest man*).

   ▶ **The motorcyclist I saw on the street was carrying** *a* **jacket and wearing black leather pants.**

34c Basic rules for articles

1. Use *the* whenever a reference to a common noun is specific and unique for writer and reader (see **34d**).

   the
   ▶ **He loves ̭house that she bought.**

2. Do not use *a/an* with plural countable nouns.

▶ They cited ~~a~~ reliable surveys.

3. Do not use *a/an* with uncountable nouns.

▶ He gave ~~a~~ helpful advice.

4. To make generalizations about countable nouns, do one of the following:
   - Use the plural form: *Lions are majestic.*
   - Use the singular with *a/an*: *A lion is a majestic animal.*
   - Use the singular with *the* to denote a classification: *The lion is a majestic animal.*

5. A countable singular noun can never stand alone. Make sure that a countable singular noun is preceded by an article or by a demonstrative pronoun *(this, that)*, a numeral, a singular word expressing quantity (see **23h**), or a possessive.

   A (Every, That, One, Her) nurse
   ▶ ~~Nurse~~ has a difficult job.

6. In general, though there are many exceptions, use no article with a singular proper noun *(Mount Everest)*, and use *the* with a plural proper noun *(the Himalayas)*.

34d *The* for a specific reference

When you write a common noun that both you and the reader know refers to one or more specific persons, places, things, or concepts, use the article *the*. The reference can be specific in two ways: outside the text or inside it.

Specific reference outside the text

▶ I study the earth, the sun, and the moon. [The ones in our solar system]

▶ She closed the door. [Of the room she was in]

▶ Her husband took the dog out for a walk. [The dog belonging to the couple]

Specific reference inside the text

▶ *The* kitten that her daughter brought home had a distinctive black patch above one eye. [The kitten is identified as a specific one.]

▶ **Her daughter found *a* kitten. When they were writing a lost-and-found ad that night, they realized that *the* kitten had a distinctive black patch above one eye.**

[The second mention is to a specific kitten identified earlier—the one her daughter found.]

▶ **He bought *the most expensive* bicycle in the store.**

[A superlative makes a reference to one specific item.]

35 Infinitive, – *ing*, and – *ed* Forms

35a Verb followed by an infinitive

Some verbs are followed by an infinitive (*to* + base form): *His father wanted to rule the family.* Verbs commonly followed by an infinitive include

agree	choose	fail	offer	refuse
ask	claim	hope	plan	venture
beg	decide	manage	pretend	want
bother	expect	need	promise	wish

Note any differences between English and your own language. In Spanish, for example, the word for *refuse* is followed by the equivalent of an *-ing* form.

to criticize
▶ **He refused ~~criticizing~~ the system.**

Position of a negative   In a verb + infinitive pattern, the position of the negative affects meaning. Note the difference in meaning that the position of a negative (*not, never*) can create.

▶ **He did not decide to buy a new car. His wife did.**

▶ **He decided not to buy a new car. His wife was disappointed.**

Verb + noun or pronoun + infinitive   Some verbs are followed by a noun or pronoun and then an infinitive.

▶ **The librarian *advised me to use* a better database.**

Verbs that follow this pattern are *advise, allow, ask, encourage, expect, force, need, order, persuade, cause, command, convince, remind, require, tell, urge, want, warn.*

Languages such as Spanish and Russian use a *that* clause after verbs like *want*. In English, however, *want* is followed by an infinitive, not by a *that* clause.

> her son to
> ▶ Rose *wanted* ~~that her son would~~ become a doctor.

Make, let, *and* have After these verbs, use a noun or pronoun and a base form of the verb (without *to*).

▶ He *made his son practice* for an hour.

▶ They *let us leave* early.

▶ She *had me wash* the car.

35b Verb followed by *-ing* (gerund)

▶ I can't help *singing* along with Paul Simon.

The *-ing* form of a verb used as a noun is known as a *gerund*. The verbs that are systematically followed by an *-ing* form make up a relatively short and learnable list.

admit	consider	enjoy	miss ·	resist
appreciate	delay	finish	postpone	risk
avoid	deny	imagine	practice	suggest
be worth	discuss	keep	recall	tolerate
can't help	dislike			

> inviting
> ▶ We considered ~~to invite~~ his parents.

> reading
> ▶ He dislikes ~~to read~~ in bed.

Note that a negation comes between the verb and the *-ing* form:

▶ During their vacation, they enjoy *not* getting up early every day.

35c Verb followed by a preposition + *-ing*

After a preposition, use the *-ing* form that functions as a noun (the gerund).

▶ They congratulated him *on winning* the prize.

▶ He ran three miles *without stopping*.

▶ The cheese is the right consistency *for spreading*.

NOTE: Take care not to confuse *to* as a preposition with *to* used in an infinitive. When *to* is a preposition, it is followed by a noun, a pronoun, a noun phrase, or an *-ing* form, not by the base form of a verb.

▶ They want *to adopt* a child.   [infinitive]

▶ They are looking forward *to adopting* a child.
   [preposition + *-ing*]

See Glossary of Usage, page 192, for forms used after *used to* and *get used to*.

35d Verb followed by an infinitive or *-ing*

Some verbs can be followed by either an infinitive or an *-ing* form (a gerund) with almost no discernible difference in meaning: *begin, continue, hate, like, love, start.*

▶ She loves *cooking*.   ▶ She loves *to cook*.

With a few verbs, however *(forget, remember, try, stop)*, the infinitive and the *-ing* form signal different meanings:

▶ He remembered to mail the letter. [intention]

▶ He remembered mailing the letter. [past act]

35e *-ing* and *-ed* forms as adjectives

Adjectives can be formed from both the present participle *-ing* form and the past participle form of verbs (*-ed* ending for regular verbs). Each form has a different meaning: The *-ing* adjective indicates that the word modified produces an effect; the past participle adjective indicates that the word modified has an effect produced on it.

▶ The boring cook served baked beans yet again.

   [The cook produces boredom. Everyone is tired of baked beans.]

▶ The bored cook yawned as she scrambled eggs.

   [The cook felt the emotion of boredom as she did the cooking, but the eggs could still be appreciated.]

PRODUCES AN EFFECT	HAS AN EFFECT PRODUCED ON IT
amazing	amazed
amusing	amused
annoying	annoyed
confusing	confused
depressing	depressed
disappointing	disappointed
embarrassing	embarrassed
exciting	excited
interesting	interested
satisfying	satisfied
shocking	shocked
worrying	worried

NOTE: Do not drop the *-ed* ending from a past participle. Sometimes in speech it blends with a following *t* or *d* sound, but in writing the *-ed* ending must be included.

► I was surprise to see her wild outfit.

► They are suppose to meet the deadline.

36 Sentence Structure and Word Order

36a Basic rules of order

- Always include the subject of a clause, even a filler subject *it* or *there*.

  ► The critics hated the movie because was too

  sentimental.

  ► When the company lost money, were

  immediate effects on share prices.

- Do not use a pronoun to restate the subject.

    ▶ **The adviser who was recommended to me** ~~she~~
    was very helpful.

- Do not put an adverb or a phrase between the verb and
  its object.

    ▶ **The quiz show host congratulated** |many times|

    the winner.

    ▶ **He saw** |yesterday| **the movie.**

- Position a long descriptive phrase after, not before, the
  noun it modifies.

    ▶ **I would go to** |known only to me| **places.**

- Stick to the order of subject-verb-direct object.

                                E
    ▶ ~~Good grades received~~ *e*very student in the
    received good grades.
    class/ ∧

- Do not include a pronoun that a relative pronoun has
  replaced.

    ▶ **The house that I lived in** i̶t̶ **for ten years has
    been sold.**

36b Direct and indirect object

Some verbs can be followed by both a direct object and
an indirect object. (The indirect object is the person or
thing to whom or to what, or for whom or for what, something
is done.) *Give, send, show, tell, teach, find, sell, ask, offer, pay, pass,*
and *hand* are some verbs that take indirect objects. The indirect
object follows the verb and precedes the direct object.

```
      ┌── IO ──┐ ┌── DO ──┐
```
▶ **He gave his mother some flowers.**
```
       IO   ┌── DO ──┐
```
▶ **He gave her some flowers.**

An indirect object can also be replaced with a prepositional phrase that *follows* the direct object:

┌── DO ──┐ ┌─ prepositional phrase ─┐
▶ He gave some flowers to his mother.

NOTE: Some verbs—such as *explain, describe, say, mention,* and *open*—are never followed by an indirect object. However, they can be followed by a direct object and a prepositional phrase with *to* or *for:*

to me
▶ She explained ~~me~~ the election process.

to us
▶ He described ~~us~~ the menu.

36c Direct and indirect questions

When a direct question is reported indirectly, it loses the quotation marks, the word order of a question, and the question mark. Sometimes changes in tense are also necessary after an introductory verb in the past tense (see **22d**).

DIRECT QUESTION | The buyer asked, "*Are the goods* ready to be shipped?"

INDIRECT QUESTION | The buyer asked if *the goods were* ready to be shipped.

DIRECT QUESTION | "Why *did you send* a letter instead of a fax?" my boss asked.

INDIRECT QUESTION | My boss asked why *I [had] sent* a letter instead of a fax.

Use only a question word or *if* or *whether* to introduce an indirect question. Do not use *that* as well.

▶ My boss wondered ~~that~~ why I had left early.

Avoid shifts between direct and indirect quotations (**21d**).

36d *Although* and *because* clauses

In some languages, a subordinating conjunction (such as *although* or *because*) can be used along with a coordinating conjunction *(but, so)* or a transitional expression *(however, therefore)* in the same sentence. In English, only one is used.

FAULTY	*Although* he loved his father, *but* he did not visit him.
POSSIBLE REVISIONS	*Although* he loved his father, he did not visit him.
	He loved his father, *but* he did not visit him.

FAULTY	*Because* she loved children, *therefore* she became a teacher.
POSSIBLE REVISIONS	*Because* she loved children, she became a teacher.
	She loved children, *so* she became a teacher.
	She loved children; *therefore,* she became a teacher.

See **26a** for punctuation with *therefore* and other transitional expressions.

Part 8
Glossaries and Index

183

37 Glossary of Usage

accept, except, expect *Accept* is a verb: *She accepted the salary offer. Except* is usually a preposition: *Everyone has gone home except my boss. Expect* is a verb: *They expect to visit New Mexico on vacation.*

adapt, adopt *Adopt* means "to take into a family" or "to take up and follow": *The couple adopted a three-year-old child. The company adopted a more aggressive policy. Adapt* means "to adjust" and is used with the preposition *to: We need some time to adapt to work after college.*

advice, advise *Advice* is a noun: *Take my advice and don't start smoking. Advise* is a verb: *He advised his brother to stop smoking.*

affect, effect In their most common uses, *affect* is a verb, and *effect* is a noun. To *affect* is to have an *effect* on something: *Pesticides can affect health. Pesticides have a bad effect on health. Effect*, however, can be used as a verb meaning "to bring about": *The administration hopes to effect new health care legislation. Affect* can also be used as a noun in psychology, meaning "a feeling or emotion."

all ready, already *All ready* means "totally prepared": *The students were all ready for their final examination. Already* means "by this time": *He has already written the report.*

all right, alright *Alright* is nonstandard. *All right* is standard.

all together, altogether *Altogether* is an adverb meaning "totally," often used before an adjective: *His presentation was altogether impressive. All together* is used to describe acting simultaneously: *As soon as the boss appeared, the managers spoke up all together.*

allude, elude *Allude* means "to refer to": *She alluded to his height. Elude* means "to avoid": *He eluded her criticism by leaving the room.*

allusion, illusion *Allusion* means "reference to": *Her allusions to his height made him uncomfortable. Illusion* means "false idea": *He had no illusions about being Mr. Universe.*

almost, most Do not use *most* to mean *almost: Almost* (not *Most*) *all my friends are computer literate.*

a lot, alot, lots *Alot* is nonstandard. *A lot of* and *lots of* are regarded by some as informal for *many* or *a great deal of: They have performed many research studies.*

ambiguous, ambivalent *Ambiguous* is used to describe a phrase or act with more than one meaning: *The ending of the movie is ambiguous; we don't know if the butler really committed the murder.* *Ambivalent* describes lack of certainty and the coexistence of opposing attitudes and feelings: *The committee is ambivalent about the proposal for restructuring the company.*

among, between Use *between* for two items, *among* for three or more: *I couldn't decide between red or blue. I couldn't decide among red, blue, or green.*

amount, number *Number* is used with countable plural expressions: *a large number of people, a number of attempts.* *Amount* is used with uncountable expressions: *a large amount of money, work,* or *information.*

anyone, any one *Anyone* is a singular indefinite pronoun meaning "anybody": *Can anyone help me? Any one* refers to one from a group and is usually followed by *of* + plural noun: *Any one* (as opposed to any two) *of the suggestions will be considered acceptable.*

anyplace The standard *anywhere* is preferable.

anyway, anywhere, nowhere; anyways, anywheres, nowheres *Anyway, anywhere,* and *nowhere* are standard forms. The others, ending in -*s,* are not.

apart, a part *Apart* is an adverb: *The old book fell apart.* But *I'd like to be a part of that project.*

as, as if, like See *like, as, as if.*

as regards, in regard to See *in regard to, as regards.*

at Avoid including *at* at the end of a question: *Where's the library?* not *Where's the library at?*

awful, awfully Avoid using these words to mean "bad" (*It's an awful story*) or "very" (*They are awfully rich*).

a while, awhile *While* is a noun: *a while ago; in a while. Awhile* is an adverb meaning "for some time": *They lived awhile in the wilderness.*

bad, badly *Bad* is an adjective, *badly* an adverb. Use *bad* after linking verbs (such as *am, is, become, seem*); use *badly* to modify verbs: *They felt bad after losing the match. They had played badly.*

because, because of *Because* is used to introduce a dependent clause: *Because it was raining, we left early. Because of* is followed by a noun: *We left early because of the rain.*

being as, being that   Avoid. Use *because* instead: *Because* (not *Being as*) *I was tired, I didn't go to class.*

belief, believe   *Belief* is a noun: *She has radical beliefs. Believe* is a verb: *He believes in an afterlife.*

beside, besides   *Beside* is a preposition meaning "next to"; *besides* is a preposition meaning "except for": *Sit beside me. He has no assistants besides us. Besides* is also an adverb meaning "in addition": *I hate horror movies. Besides, there's a long line.*

better   See *had better.*

between   See *among.*

breath, breathe   The first is a noun, the second a verb: *Take three deep breaths. Breathe in deeply.*

can't hardly   This expression is nonstandard. See *hardly.*

cite, site, sight   *Cite* means "to quote or mention"; *site* is a noun meaning "location"; *sight* is a noun meaning "view": *She cited the page number in her paper. They visited the original site of the abbey. The sight of the skyline from the plane produced applause from the passengers.*

complement, compliment   As verbs, *complement* means "to complete or add to something," and *compliment* means "to make a flattering comment about someone or something": *The wine complemented the meal. The guests complimented the hostess on the fine dinner.* As nouns, the words have meanings associated with the verbs: *The wine was a fine complement to the meal. The guests paid the hostess a compliment.*

compose, comprise   *Compose* means "to make up"; *comprise* means "to include." *The conference center is composed of twenty-five rooms. The conference center comprises twenty-five rooms.*

conscience, conscious   *Conscience* is a noun meaning "awareness of right and wrong." *Conscious* is an adjective meaning "awake" or "aware." *Her conscience troubled her after the accident. The victim was still not conscious.*

continual, continuous   *Continual* implies repetition, while *continuous* implies lack of a pause. *The continual interruptions made the lecturer angry. Continuous rain for two hours stopped play.*

could care less   This expression used without a negative is not standard. In formal English, use it only with a negative: *They couldn't care less about their work.*

custom, customs, costume   *Custom* means "habitual practice or tradition." *Customs* refers to a government agency that collects taxes on imports or to the procedures for inspecting items entering a country. A *costume* is a style of dress: *a family custom; go through customs at the airport; a Halloween costume.*

dairy, diary   The first is associated with cows and milk, the second with daily journal writing.

desert, dessert   *Desert* can be pronounced two ways and can be a noun with the stress on the first syllable *(the Mojave Desert)* or a verb, pronounced the same way as the noun *dessert: When did he desert his family?* As a noun, *desert* means "a dry, often sandy, environment." As a verb *desert* means "to abandon." *Dessert* (with the stress on the second syllable) is the sweet course at the end of a meal.

different from, different than   Standard usage is *different from: She looks different from her sister.* However, *different than* appears frequently in speech and informal writing, particularly when *different from* would require more words: *My writing is different than* (in place of *different from what*) *it was last semester.*

disinterested, uninterested   *Disinterested* means "impartial or unbiased": *The mediator was hired to make a disinterested settlement. Uninterested* means "lacking in interest": *He seemed so uninterested in his job that his boss wondered what to do about him.*

due to   Use *due to*, not *because of,* after a noun plus a form of *be: The Yankees' win was due to Wells's pitching.* See also *because, because of.*

due to the fact that, owing to the fact that   Wordy. Use *because* instead: *They stopped the game because* (not *due to the fact that*) *it was raining.*

each, every   These are singular pronouns; use them with a singular verb. See also **23d** and **23g**.

each other, one another   Use *each other* with two, *one another* with more than two: *The twins love each other. The triplets all love one another.*

effect   See *affect.*

e.g.   In the body of a formal text, use *for example* or *for instance* in place of this Latin abbreviation.

elicit, illicit   *Elicit* means "to get or draw out": *The police tried in vain to elicit information from the suspect's accomplice. Illicit* is an adjective meaning "illegal": *Their illicit deals landed them in prison.*

elude   See *allude, elude.*

emigrate, immigrate   *Emigrate from* is "to leave a country"; *immigrate to* is "to move to another country": *They emigrated from the Ukraine and immigrated to the United States.* The noun forms *emigrant* and *immigrant* are derived from the verbs.

eminent, imminent   *Eminent* means "well known and noteworthy": *an eminent lawyer; imminent* means "about to happen": *an imminent disaster.*

etc.   This abbreviation for the Latin *et cetera* means "and so on." Do not let a list trail off with *etc.* Rather than *They took a tent, a sleeping bag, etc.,* write *They took a tent, a sleeping bag, cooking utensils, and a stove.*

every, each   See *each, every.*

everyday, every day   *Everyday* as one word is an adjective meaning "usual": *Their everyday routine is to break for lunch at 12:30. Every day* is an adverbial expression of frequency: *I get up early every day.*

except, expect   See *accept, except, expect.*

explicit, implicit   *Explicit* means "direct": *She gave explicit instructions. Implicit* means "implied": *A tax increase is implicit in the proposal.*

farther, further   Both can apply to distance: *She lives farther (further) from the campus than I do.* But only *further* is used to mean "additional" or "additionally": *The management offered further incentives. Further, the union proposed new work rules.*

female, male   Use these words as adjectives, not as nouns replacing *man* and *woman: There are only three women* (not *females*) *in my class. We are discussing female conversational traits.*

few, a few   Use *a few* for *some;* use *few* for *hardly any: She has a few days off to relax. She has few friends and is lonely.*

fewer, less   Formal usage demands *fewer* with plural countable nouns (*fewer holidays*), *less* with uncountable nouns (*less money*). However, in informal usage, *less* with plural nouns commonly occurs, especially with *than: less than six items, less than ten miles, fifty words or less.* In formal usage, *fewer* is preferred.

get married to, marry   These expressions can be used interchangeably: *She will marry her childhood friend next month. He will get married to his fiancée next week.* (The noun form is *marriage: Their marriage has lasted thirty years.*)

had better   Include the *had* in standard English, although it is often omitted in advertising and in speech: *You had better* (not *You better*) *try harder.*

hardly   This is a negative word. Do not use it with another negative: *He could hardly walk* (not *He couldn't hardly walk*) *after the accident.*

hisself   Nonstandard; use *himself.*

illicit, elicit   See *elicit, illicit.*

illusion, allusion   See *allusion, illusion.*

immigrate, emigrate   See *emigrate, immigrate.*

imminent, eminent   See *eminent, imminent.*

implicit   See *explicit, implicit.*

imply, infer   *Imply* means "to suggest in an indirect way": *He implied that further layoffs were unlikely. Infer* means "to guess" or "to draw a conclusion": *I inferred that the company was doing well.*

incredible, incredulous   *Incredible* means "difficult to believe": *The violence of the storm was incredible. Incredulous* means "skeptical, unable to believe": *They were incredulous when he told them about his daring exploits in the whitewater rapids.*

in regard to, as regards   Use one or the other. Do not use the nonstandard *in regards to.*

irregardless   Avoid this nonstandard form and use *regardless* instead: *He selected history as a major regardless of the preparation it would give him for a career.*

it's, its   The apostrophe in *it's* signals not a possessive but a contraction of *it is* or *it has. Its* is the possessive form of the pronoun *it: The city government agency has produced its final report. It's available upon request.* See also **27d**.

kind, sort, type   In the singular, use with *this* and a singular noun. Use in the plural with *these* and a plural noun: *this kind of book; these kinds of books.*

kind of, sort of   Do not use these to mean "somewhat" or "a little": *The pace of the baseball game was somewhat* (not *kind of*) *slow.*

lend, loan   *Lend* is a verb, but *loan* is ordinarily used as a noun: *Our cousins offered to lend us some money, but we refused the loan.*

less, fewer   See *fewer, less.*

like, as, as if   *As* and *as if* introduce a dependent clause with a subject and verb: *She walks as her father does. She looks as if she could eat a big meal. Like* is a preposition followed by a noun or pronoun, not by a clause: *She looks like her father.* In speech, however, *like* is often used where formal usage dictates *as* or *as*

if: She walks like her father does. He looks like he needs a new suit.
Formal usage requires *He looks as if he needs a new suit.*

loan　See *lend, loan.*

loose, lose　*Loose* is an adjective meaning the opposite of *tight: This jacket is comfortable because it is so loose. Lose* is a verb, with the past tense and past participle form *lost: Many people lose their jobs in a recession.*

lot, alot, lots　See *a lot, alot, lots.*

marital, martial　*Marital* is associated with marriage, *martial* with war.

may be, maybe　*May be* consists of a modal verb followed by the base form of the verb *be; maybe* is an adverb meaning "perhaps." If you can replace the expression with *perhaps*, make it one word: *They may be there already, or maybe they got caught in traffic.*

most, almost　See *almost, most.*

myself　Use only as a reflexive pronoun (*I told them myself*) or as an intensive pronoun (*I myself told them*). Do not use *myself* as a subject pronoun; use *My sister and I won* (not *My sister and myself won*).

nowadays　All one word. Make sure you include the final *-s.*

nowhere, nowheres　See *anyway.*

number, amount　See *amount, number.*

of a　Do not use *of a* after an adjective. Omit *of: She's not that good a player* (not *She's not that good of a player*).

off, off of　Use only *off*, not *off of: She drove the car off the road* (not *off of*).

OK, O.K., okay　Reserve these forms for informal speech and writing. Choose another word in a formal context: *Her performance was satisfactory* (in place of *Her performance was OK*).

one another　See *each other, one another.*

owing to the fact that　See *due to the fact that.*

passed, past　*Passed* is a past tense verb form: *They passed the deli on the way to work. He passed his exam. Past* can be a noun (*in the past*), an adjective (*in past times*), or a preposition (*She walked past the bakery*).

plus　Do not use *plus* as a coordinating conjunction or a transitional expression. Use *and* or *moreover* instead: *He was promoted and* (not *plus*) *he received a bonus.* Use *plus* as a preposition meaning "in addition to": *His salary plus his dividends placed him in a high tax bracket.*

precede, proceed *Precede* means "to go or occur before": *The Roaring Twenties preceded the Great Depression. Proceed* means "to go ahead": *After you have paid the fee, proceed to the examination room.*

pretty Avoid using *pretty* as an intensifying adverb. Omit it or use a word like *really, very, rather,* or *quite: The stew tastes very* (not *pretty*) *good.*

principal, principle *Principal* is a noun *(the principal of a school)* or an adjective meaning "main": *His principal motive was greed. Principle* is a noun meaning "standard or rule": *He always acts on his principles.*

quite, quiet Do not confuse the adverb *quite,* meaning "very," with the adjective *quiet* ("still" or "silent"): *We felt quite relieved when the audience became quiet.*

quote, quotation *Quote* is a verb. Do not use it as a noun; use *quotation: The quotation* (not *quote*) *from Walker tells the reader a great deal.*

real, really *Real* is an adjective; *really* is an adverb. Do not use *real* as an intensifying adverb: *She acted really* (not *real*) *well.*

reason is because Avoid *the reason is because.* Instead, use *the reason is that* or rewrite the sentence. See **21g.**

regardless See *irregardless.*

respectable, respectful, respective *Respectable* means "presentable, worthy of respect": *Wear some respectable shoes to your interview. Respectful* means "polite or deferential": *Parents want their children to be respectful to adults. Respective* means "particular" or "individual": *The friends of the bride and the groom sat in their respective seats in the church.*

should (could, might, etc.) of Nonstandard for *should have tried; might have seen.*

since Use only when time or reason is clear: *Since you insist on helping, I'll let you paint this bookcase.* Unclear: *Since he got a new job, he has been happy.*

site, sight, cite See *cite, site, sight.*

sometimes, sometime, some time *Sometimes* means "occasionally": *He sometimes prefers to eat lunch at his desk. Sometime* means "at an indefinite time": *I read that book sometime last year.* The expression *some time* is the noun *time* modified by the quantity word *some: I worked for Honda for some time—about five years, I think.*

sort, type, kind See *kind, sort, type.*

sort of, kind of See *kind of, sort of.*

stationary, stationery *Stationary* means "not moving" (*a stationary vehicle*); you use *stationery* when you write letters.

than, then *Then* is a time word; *than* must be preceded by a comparative form: *bigger than, more interesting than.*

their, there, they're *They're* is a contracted form of *they are; there* indicates place or is used as a filler in the subject position in a sentence; *their* is a pronoun indicating possession: *They're over there, guarding their luggage.*

theirself, theirselves, themself Nonstandard; use *themselves.*

to, too, two Do not confuse these words. *To* is a sign of the infinitive and a common preposition; *too* is an adverb; *two* is the number: *She is too smart to agree to report to two bosses.*

uninterested, disinterested See *disinterested, uninterested.*

used to, get (become) used to These expressions share the common form *used to.* But the first, expressing a past habit that no longer exists, is followed by a base form of the verb: *He used to wear his hair long.* (Note that after *not,* the form is *use to: He did not use to have a beard.*) In the expression *get (become) used to, used to* means "accustomed to" and is followed by a noun or an *-ing* form: *She couldn't get used to driving on the left when she was in England.*

way, ways Use *way* to mean "distance": *He has a way to go. Ways* in this context is nonstandard.

weather, whether *Weather* is a noun; *whether* is a conjunction: *The weather will determine whether we go on the picnic.*

whose, who's *Whose* is possessive: *Whose goal was that? Who's* is a contraction of *who is* or *who has: Who's the player whose pass was caught?*

your, you're *Your* is a pronoun used to show possession. *You're* is a contraction for *you are: You're wearing your new shoes today, aren't you?*

38 Glossary of Grammatical Terms

absolute phrase A phrase consisting of a noun followed by a participle (*-ing* or past participle) and modifying an entire sentence: *The flags blowing in the wind,* the stadium looked bleak. **26d.**

active voice   Attribute of a verb when its grammatical subject performs the action: The dog *ate* the cake. See also *passive voice*.

adjective   A word that describes or limits (modifies) a noun or pronoun: A *happy* child. The child is *happy*. **25**. See also *comparative, coordinate adjective, superlative*.

adjective clause   See *relative clause*.

adverb   A word that modifies a verb, an adjective, or another adverb. Many adverbs end in *-ly:* She ran *quickly*. He is *really* successful. The children were *well* liked. **25**. See also *comparative, superlative*.

adverb clause   A dependent clause that modifies a verb, an adjective, or an adverb and begins with a subordinating conjunction: He left early *because he was tired*.

agreement   The grammatical match in person, number, and gender between a verb and its subject or a pronoun and the word it refers to (its *antecedent*): The *benefits continue; they are* pleasing. The *benefit continues. It is* pleasing. **23, 24c**.

antecedent   The noun that a pronoun refers to or replaces: My sons found a *kitten. It* was black and white. **24b, 24c**.

appositive phrase   A phrase occurring next to a noun and used to describe it: His father, *a factory worker*, is running for office. **24a**.

article   *A, an* (indefinite articles), or *the* (definite article). **34** ESL.

auxiliary verb   A verb that joins with another verb to form a complete verb. Auxiliary verbs are forms of *do, be*, and *have*, as well as the modal auxiliary verbs. **22a, 22b**. See also *modal auxiliary verb*.

base form   The form of a verb with no endings; the dictionary form, used in an infinitive after *to: see, eat, go, be*. **22a**.

clause   A group of words that includes a subject and a verb. See also *independent clause; dependent clause*. **19, 20, 26a, 26b**.

cliché   An overused, predictable expression: *as cool as a cucumber*. **18a**.

collective noun   A noun naming a group of people, places, objects, or ideas that are regarded as a unit: *society, jury, family*. **23e, 24c**.

comma splice   An error caused by connecting two independent clauses with only a comma. **20**.

common noun   A noun that does not name a unique person, place, or thing. **34a** ESL. See also *proper noun*.

comparative The form of an adjective or adverb used to compare two people or things: *bigger, more interesting.* **25e.**

complement A *subject complement* is a word or group of words used after a linking verb to refer to and describe the subject: Harry looks *happy.* An *object complement* is a word or group of words used after a direct object to complete its meaning: They call him a *liar.* **25b.**

complete verb A verb that shows tense. Some verb forms, such as present (*-ing*) participles and past participles, require an auxiliary verb or verbs to make them complete verbs. *Going* and *seen* are not complete verbs; *are going* and *has been seen* are complete. **22a.**

compound adjective An adjective formed of two or more words, used as one unit, and often connected with hyphens: a *well-constructed* house. **25c.**

compound noun A noun formed of two or more words: *toothbrush, merry-go-round.* **32b.**

compound predicate A predicate containing two or more verbs and their objects, complements, and modifiers: He *whistles* and *sings in the morning.* **19c, 26b.**

compound subject Two subjects with the same predicate and the parts of the subject joined by words such as *and, or,* and *nor*: *My uncle and my aunt* are leaving soon. **23f.**

conditional clause A clause introduced by *if* or *unless,* expressing conditions of fact, prediction, or speculation: *If we earn more, we spend more.* **22f.**

conjunction A word or words like *and* and *because* joining sentences or sentence elements. See also *coordinating conjunction, subordinating conjunction.* **19b, 20b.**

contraction A word or words abbreviated by replacing one or more letters with an apostrophe: *can't* (for *cannot*), *he's* (for *he is* or *he has*), or *they're* (for *they are*). **27a, 27d.**

coordinate adjective One of two or more evaluative adjectives modifying the same noun or pronoun. When coordinate adjectives appear in a series, their order can be reversed and they can be separated by *and.* Commas are used between coordinate adjectives: the *comfortable, expensive car.* **26a.**

coordinating conjunction The seven coordinating conjunctions are *and, but, or, nor, so, for,* and *yet.* They connect sentence elements that are parallel in structure: He couldn't call, *but* he wrote a letter. **20b, 26a, 26b, 31a.**

countable noun   A common noun that has a plural form and can be used after a plural quantity word (*many, three,* and so on); one *book,* three *stores,* many *children.* **34a** ESL.

dangling modifier   A modifier that does not clearly modify the noun or pronoun it is intended to modify. *Turning the corner,* the lights went out. (Corrected: *Turning the corner, we* saw the lights go out.) **21c.**

demonstrative pronoun   *This, that, these,* or *those: That* is my glass. **24c.**

dependent clause   A clause that cannot stand alone as a complete sentence and needs to be attached to an independent clause. A dependent clause begins with a subordinating word such as *because, if, when, although, who, which,* or *that: When it rains,* we can't take the children outside. **19b.**

diction   Choice of appropriate words and tone. **18.**

direct object   The person or thing that receives the action of a verb or verb form: They ate *cake* and *ice cream.* **36b** ESL.

direct quotation   A person's words, reproduced exactly by a writer and placed in quotation marks: *"I won't be home until noon,"* she said. **8a, 21d, 26a, 36c** ESL.

double negative   Using two negative words in the same sentence is nonstandard usage: I do *not* know *nothing.* (Corrected: I do not know anything.) **25d.**

dummy subject   See *filler subject.*

ellipsis   Omission of words from a quotation, indicated by three dots (an *ellipsis mark*): "I pledge allegiance to the flag . . . and to the republic for which it stands. . . ." **8a, 29e.**

faulty predication   A construction in which subject and verb do not fit logically: The *decrease* in stolen cars *has diminished* in the past year. (Corrected: The *number* of stolen cars *has decreased* in the past year.) **21e.**

filler (or dummy) subject   *It* or *there* used in the subject position of a clause, followed by a form of *be: There are* two elm trees on the corner. **15b, 23c.**

first person   The person speaking or writing: *I* or *we.* **24a.**

fragment   A group of words that is punctuated as a sentence but is grammatically incomplete because it lacks a subject or a complete verb or lacks an independent clause: *Because it was a sunny day.* **19.**

fused sentence   See *run-on sentence.*

gender Classification of a noun or pronoun as masculine *(Uncle John, he)*, feminine *(Ms. Torez, she)*, or neuter *(book, it)*. **18c, 24c.**

generic noun A noun referring to a general class or type of person or object: A *student* has to write many papers. **24c.**

gerund A form, derived from a verb, that ends in *-ing* and functions as a noun: *Walking* is good for your health. **23d, 24a, 35b ESL, 35c ESL.**

helping verb See *auxiliary verb.*

indefinite pronoun A pronoun that refers to a nonspecific person or object: *anybody, something.* **23g.**

independent clause A clause containing a subject and a complete verb, not introduced by a subordinating word. An independent clause stands alone grammatically: *Birds sing. The old man was singing a song.* Hailing a cab, *the woman used a silver whistle.* **19, 20, 26a, 26b.**

indirect object The person or thing to whom or what, or for whom or what, an action is performed. It comes between a verb and a direct object: He gave his *sister* some flowers. **36b ESL.**

indirect question A question reported by a speaker or writer, with no quotation marks: They asked *if we would help them.* **36c ESL.**

indirect quotation A presentation or paraphrase of the words of another speaker or writer, integrated into a writer's own sentence: He said *that they were making money.* **21d.**

infinitive The base form, or dictionary form, of a verb, preceded by *to: to see, to steal.* **31a, 35a ESL, 35d ESL.**

intransitive verb A verb that is not followed by a direct object: Exciting events *have occurred.* He *fell.* **22c, 22d, 22g.** See also *transitive verb.*

irregular verb A verb that does not form its past tense and past participle with *-ed: sing, sang, sung.* **22a.**

linking verb A verb connecting a subject to its complement. Typical linking verbs are *be, become, seem,* and *appear:* He *seems* angry. A linking verb is intransitive; it does not take a direct object. **24a, 25b.**

mental activity verb A verb not used in a tense showing progressive aspect: *prefer, want, understand:* He *wants* to leave (*not* He *is wanting*). **22d.**

misplaced modifier An adverb (particularly *only* and *even*) or a descriptive phrase or clause positioned in a sentence in such a way that it appears to modify the wrong word or words: She showed the doll to her sister *that her aunt gave her.* **21b.**

mixed structure   A sentence with two or more types of structures that do not match grammatically: *By doing* her homework at the last minute *caused* Meg to make many mistakes. **21a.**

modal auxiliary verb   An auxiliary verb used with the base form of the main verb. Modal auxiliaries are seldom used alone and do not change form. The modal auxiliaries are *will, would, can, could, shall, should, may, might,* and *must.* **22b.**

modifier   A word or words that describe a noun, verb, phrase, or whole clause: He is a *happy* man. He is smiling *happily.* **21b, 25.**

mood   The mood of a verb tells whether it states a fact (*indicative:* She *goes* to school); gives a command (*imperative: Come* back soon); or expresses a condition, wish, or request (*subjunctive:* I wish you *were* not leaving). **22f.**

nonrestrictive phrase or clause   A phrase or clause that adds nonessential information to a sentence. It is set off with commas: His report, *which he gave to his boss yesterday,* received enthusiastic praise. Also called *nonessential phrase* or *clause.* **24e, 26c.**

noun   A word that names a person, place, thing, or idea. Nouns can be proper or common and, if common, countable or uncountable. **34a ESL.** See also the following entries on the various types of nouns: *collective noun, common noun, compound noun, countable noun, generic noun, proper noun, uncountable noun.*

number   The indication of a noun or pronoun as singular (one person, place, thing, or idea) or plural (more than one). **23a, 24a.**

object of preposition   A noun or pronoun (along with its modifiers) following a preposition: on *the beach.* **35c ESL.**

paragraph   A group of sentences, usually on one topic, set off in a text. **1, 16d.**

parallelism   The use of coordinate structures that have the same grammatical form: She likes *swimming* and *playing* tennis. **21f.**

participle phrase   A phrase beginning with a present participle (*-ing*) or a past participle: The woman *wearing a green skirt* is my sister. *Baffled by the puzzle,* he gave up. **21c.**

passive voice   Attribute of a verb when its grammatical subject is the receiver of the action that the verb describes: The book *was written* by my professor. **15c, 22g.** See also *active voice.*

past participle   A form of a verb, ending in -*ed* for regular verbs and having various forms for irregular verbs. The past participle needs an auxiliary verb or verbs in order to function as a complete verb of a clause: *has chosen, was cleaned, might have been told*. It can also function alone as an adjective. **22a, 22e, 22g, 35e** ESL.

perfect progressive verb tense forms   Verb tenses that show actions in progress up to a specific point in present, past, or future time. For active voice verbs, use a form of the auxiliary *have been* followed by the -*ing* form of the verb: *has/have been living, had been living, will have been living*. **22d.**

perfect verb tense forms   Verb tenses that show actions completed by present, past, or future time. For active voice verbs, use forms of the auxiliary *have* followed by the past participle of the verb: *has/have arrived, had arrived, will have arrived*. **22d.**

person   The form of a pronoun or verb that indicates whether the subject is doing the speaking (first person, *I* or *we*); is spoken to (second person, *you*); or is spoken about (third person, *he, she, it*, or *they*). **24a, 24b.**

phrase   A group of words that does not contain a subject and verb but that functions as a noun, verb, adjective, or adverb: *under the tree, to work hard*. **19a.** See also *absolute phrase, appositive phrase*, and *participle phrase*.

possessive   The form of a noun or pronoun that indicates ownership. Possessive pronouns include *my, his, their*, and *theirs*. The possessive form of a noun is indicated by an apostrophe or an apostrophe and -*s: Mario's* car, the *children's* nanny, the *birds'* nests. **24a, 27a, 27b.**

predicate   The part of a sentence that contains the verb and its modifiers and that comments on or makes an assertion about the subject. **21e.**

preposition   A word used before a noun or pronoun to indicate time, space, or some other relationship (such as *in, to, for, about, during*). **31a, 35c** ESL.

present participle   The -*ing* form of a verb, showing an action in progress or as continuous: They are *sleeping*. Without an auxiliary, the -*ing* form cannot be a complete verb, but it can be used as an adjective: *searing* heat. **22a, 35e** ESL.

progressive verb tense forms   Verb tenses that show actions in progress at a point or over a period of time in past, present, or future time. They use a form of *be* + the -*ing* form of the verb: They *are working*; he *will be writing*. **22a.**

pronoun   A word used to represent a noun or a noun phrase. Pronouns are of various types: personal *(I, they)*; possessive *(my, mine, their, theirs)*; demonstrative *(this, that, these, those)*; intensive or reflexive *(myself, herself)*; relative *(who, whom, whose, which, that)*; interrogative *(who, which, what)*; and indefinite *(anyone, something)*. **23g, 24, 36a** ESL.

pronoun reference   The connection between a pronoun and its antecedent. Reference should be clear and unambiguous: The *lawyer* picked up *his* hat and left. **24b**.

proper noun   The capitalized name of a specific person, place, or thing: *Golden Gate Park, University of Kansas.* **31a, 34a** ESL.

quantity word   A word expressing the idea of quantity, such as *each, several, some, many,* or *much.* Subject-verb agreement is important with quantity words: *Each* of the students *has* a different assignment. **23h**. See also *agreement.*

reflexive pronoun   A pronoun ending in *-self* or *-selves* and referring to the subject of a clause. Standard forms are *himself* and *themselves.* See *hisself* in Glossary of Usage, page 189.

regular verb   Verb with *-ed* in past tense and past participle forms. **22a**.

relative clause   Also called an *adjective clause,* a relative clause is a dependent clause beginning with a relative pronoun *(who, whom, whose, which,* or *that)* and modifying a noun or pronoun: The writer *who won the prize* was elated. **23i, 24e**.

relative pronoun   Pronoun that introduces a relative clause: *who, whom, whose, which, that.* **23i, 24e**.

restrictive phrase or clause   A phrase or clause that provides information necessary to the identity of the word or phrase it modifies. A restrictive phrase or clause is not set off with commas: The book *that is first on the bestseller list* is a memoir. Also called *essential phrase or clause.* **24e, 26c**.

run-on sentence   Two independent clauses not separated by a conjunction or by any punctuation. Also called *fused sentence: The dog ate the meat the cat ate the fish.* (Corrected: *The dog ate the meat; the cat ate the fish.*) **20**.

second person   The person addressed: *you.* **24a, 24d**.

shifts   Inappropriate switches in grammatical structure, such as from one tense to another or between statement and command or between indirect and direct quotation: Joan asked *whether I was warm enough* and *did I sleep well.* (Corrected: ... *and slept well.*) **21d**.

split infinitive An infinitive with a word or words inserted between *to* and the base form of the verb: *to successfully complete*. Some readers may object to this structure. **21b**.

standard English "The variety of English that is most widely accepted as the spoken and written language of educated speakers in formal and informal contexts and is characterized by generally accepted conventions of spelling, grammar, and vocabulary while admitting some regional differences, especially in pronunciation and vocabulary."—*American Heritage Dictionary*.

subject The noun or pronoun that performs the action of the verb in an active voice sentence or receives the action of the verb in a passive voice sentence. Every sentence needs a subject and a verb. **15a, 16a, 19c, 21c, 21e, 23**.

subjunctive See *mood*.

subordinate clause See *dependent clause*.

subordinating conjunction A word used to introduce a dependent adverb clause, such as *because, if, when, although, since, while*. **19b, 26b**.

superlative The form of an adjective or adverb used to compare three or more people or things: *biggest; most unusual; least effectively*. **25e**.

tense The form of a verb that indicates time. Verbs change form to distinguish present and past time: He *goes*; he *went*. Auxiliary verbs indicate progressive and perfect actions. **22d**. See also *perfect, progressive*, and *perfect progressive verb tense forms*.

third person The person or thing spoken about: *he, she, it, they*, or nouns. **24a**.

transitional expression A word or phrase used to connect two independent clauses. Typical transitional expressions are *for example, however*, and *similarly*: We were able to swim today; *in addition*, we took the canoe out on the river. A semicolon frequently occurs between the two independent clauses. **16b, 20, 26a, 29b**.

transitive verb A verb that has an object, a person or thing that receives the action (in the active voice): Dogs *chase* cats. Transitive verbs can be used in the passive voice (in which case the subject receives the action of the verb): Cats *are chased* by dogs. **22c, 22g**. See also *intransitive verb*.

uncountable noun A common noun that cannot follow a plural quantity word (such as *several* or *many*) is never used with *a* or *an*, is used with a singular third person verb, and has no plural form: *furniture, happiness, information.* **23d, 23h, 34a ESL, 34b ESL, 34c ESL.**

verb   A word that expresses action or being and that tells what the subject of the clause is or does. A complete verb of a clause might require auxiliary or modal auxiliary verbs to complete its meaning. **22.** See also the following entries for more specific information.

active voice	linking verb	perfect verb tense
agreement	mental activity	forms
auxiliary verb	verb	predicate
base form	modal auxiliary	present participle
complete verb	verb	progressive verb
compound	mood	tense forms
predicate	passive voice	regular verb
infinitive	past participle	tense
intransitive verb	perfect progres-	transitive verb
irregular verb	sive verb tense	voice
	forms	

voice   Transitive verbs (those followed by an object) can be used in the active voice (*He is painting the door*) or the passive voice (*The door is being painted*). **22g.**

zero article   The lack of an article (*a, an,* or *the*) before a noun. Uncountable nouns are used with the zero article when they make no specific reference. **34b ESL, 34c ESL.**

Index

Note: An asterisk (*) refers to a page number in the Glossary of Grammatical Terms.

An asterisk (*) refers to a page number in the Glossary of Grammatical Terms.

An asterisk (*) refers to a page number in the Glossary of Grammatical Terms.

An asterisk (*) refers to a page number in the Glossary of Grammatical Terms.

An asterisk (*) refers to a page number in the Glossary of Grammatical Terms.

An asterisk (*) refers to a page number in the Glossary of Grammatical Terms.

An asterisk (*) refers to a page number in the Glossary of Grammatical Terms.

Text Credits

American Heritage Dictionary of the English Language, 3rd ed. Definition of "Standard English." Boston: Houghton Mifflin Company, 1996. Copyright © 1996 by Houghton Mifflin Company. Reproduced by permission from *The American Heritage Dictionary of the English Language,* Third Edition.

Larkin, Philip. "Toads." *The Less Deceived, Philip Larkin: Collected Poems.* Ed. Anthony Thwaite. London: Marvell, 1989. By permission of the Marvell Press, England and Australia.

Morales, Aurora Levins. "Class Poem." *Getting Home Alive.* Ed. Aurora Morales and Rosario Morales. Ithaca, N.Y.: Firebrand. 45–47. Copyright © 1986 by Aurora Levins Morales. Used with permission from Firebrand Books, Ithaca, N.Y.

KEY POINTS BOXES

Common Correction and Editing Marks

Note: Numbers refer to sections in the book.

Abbreviation	Meaning
ab or abbr	abbreviation, 31b, 33d
adj	adjective, 25
adv	adverb, 25
agr	agreement, 23, 24c
art	article, 34
awk	awkward, 15, 16, 21
bias	biased language, 18c, 24c
case	case, 24a
cap (t̲om)	use a capital letter, 31a, 33c
comp	comparison, 21a, 25e, 25f
coord	coordination, 26a
cs	comma splice, 20
dic	diction, 18
db neg	double negative, 25d
dm	dangling modifier, 21c
doc	documentation, 10-13
-ed	error in -ed ending, 22e
frag	sentence fragment, 19
fs	fused sentence, 20
hyph	hyphenation, 32, 33c
inc	incomplete, 21h, 36a
ind quot	indirect quotation, 21d, 22d, 36c
-ing	-ing error, 35
ital	italics/underlining, 30, 33b
jar	jargon, 18b
lc (Me)	use a lowercase letter, 31a
mix or mixed	mixed construction, 21a
mm	misplaced modifier, 21b
ms	manuscript form, 3, 10d, 11d
num	faulty use of numbers, 31c

Abbreviation	Meaning
p	punctuation error, 26-29, 33
pass	ineffective passive voice, 15c, 22g
pron	pronoun error, 24
quot	quotation error, 8a, 8b
ref	pronoun reference error, 24b
rel cl	relative clause, 24e, 26c
rep	repetitive, 14a
-s	error in -s ending, 23a
shift	needless shift, 21d
sp	spelling, 1, 3c
s/pl	singular/plural error, 23a, 34a
sub	subordination, 26b, 36d
sup	superlative, 25e
s-v agr	subject-verb agreement, 23
trans	transition, 16b, 16d
und	underlining/italics, 30, 33b
usg	usage error, 37
vb	verb error, 22
vt	verb tense, 22d
wdy	wordy, 14
wo	word order, 36
ww	wrong word, 18

Symbol	Meaning
??	unclear
¶ or par	new paragraph
no ¶	no new paragraph
//	parallelism
⌒	close up space
#	add space
∧	insert
ℓ	delete
∽	transpose
✗	obvious error
⊙	needs a period
stet	do not change

Table of Contents